August 23, 1992

To Us -

We've both grown this year and
have had to stretch sometimes, too.
I think the beauty of our relationship
is in its openness. I hope that
never changes.

Happy 6th Anniversary.
Love -
Susan

OTHER GARY SMALLEY PRODUCTS FROM WORD PUBLISHING

BOOKS

The Language Of Love † ✍   HC   084-9905-575

AUDIO

How To Meet Your Husband's Needs   LLF 201-0844-009
The Incredible Worth Of A Woman   LLF 201-0255-739
The Key To Your Child's Heart   LLF 201-0247-736
The Blessing ✍   BTX 201-0522-001
The Language Of Love ✍   BTX 201-0527-003
Love Is A Decision   BTX 201-0536-002

†   Focus on the Family Publishing

✍   Co-authored with John Trent

LOVE IS A DECISION

GARY SMALLEY
WITH JOHN TRENT

WORD PUBLISHING
Dallas·London·Vancouver·Melbourne

Library of Congress Cataloging-in-Publication Data

Smalley, Gary.
    Love is a Decision.

    1. Marriage—United States. 2. Marriage—Religious
aspects—Christianity. I. Trent, John T.
II. Title.
HQ734.S686   1989   646.7'8   89–22414
ISBN 0–8499—0721–7
ISBN 0–8499–3362–5 (pbk)

Printed in the United States of America

    239   L B   9 8 7 6 5 ·

The material in this book is based largely on the "Love Is a Decision" Seminar, and its success is due largely to the efforts of Terry Brown, our national seminar director.

This book is gratefully dedicated to

Terry

Without knowing it, thousands of couples' lives have been enriched by his years of faithful, loyal service in coordinating the many details for the seminar. We thank God for this special servant and for the unique way he enriches everyone who knows him.

Contents

1

Planning on a Great Marriage?

It was just turning dark when I arrived at the home of a family I was staying with in Tampa, Florida. Exhausted after speaking at a seminar all day, I was looking forward to a restful, uneventful night.

I knew my hosts only slightly, but they lived in a beautiful home in a peaceful neighborhood. But then again, looks can be deceiving. In fact, I would never have expected either event that happened to me over the next few hours.

As I walked up to the front door, I reached into one pocket, then another. That's when I realized I'd left my key inside in my room, and I was locked out of the house. Ringing the doorbell wouldn't have done any good. My hosts had told me they wouldn't be home until late. So I decided to go around to the back yard and see if by chance a window or door had been left open.

As I rounded the back corner, I froze in terror. From out of the dark, a huge black form was racing toward me at breakneck speed. It was the biggest dog I'd ever seen in my life!

Ten feet from where I stood petrified with fear, the dog left the ground with a tremendous leap—and I knew I'd soon be on my way to the hospital. In milli-seconds I'd feel the pain of his teeth tearing into me.

I closed my eyes and braced myself for the collision . . . but nothing happened. At first I thought, *He's toying with me. This dog knows I'm about to die, and he wants to watch me suffer!* But after a moment more, I finally built up enough courage to open my eyes. Unbelievably, he was sitting happily at my feet, his big friendly tongue hanging out and his tail wagging. He was actually whimpering for me to reach down and pet him.

After my heart rate dropped from triple to double digits, I checked the house only to find it securely locked. It was getting late, and I was worn out. I was faced with either camping out on the back porch with my new-found canine friend or thinking of some alternative. That's when an idea hit me.

Another family I'd been introduced to lived in Tampa. Perhaps I could stay with them until my hosts returned. So I jumped into my car and drove across town to John and Kay Hammer's stately home—and into an even more surprising situation.

As I knocked on the door, I was greeted by Kay. "Hi, Gary," she said, flashing her million-dollar smile. She makes anyone she meets feel special and important. I explained my situation to her and John, and they insisted that I stay at their house for the night.

I met their charming children as they piled out of their rooms. Finally, after a little small talk in the living room, we all retired for the night.

My body must have known that my plane didn't leave until the next evening, because it overruled the alarm clock, and I slept late the next morning. By the time I got up, showered, and dressed, the kids and John had already headed off to school and work. Only Kay was left in the kitchen to play short-order cook for her unexpected house guest.

I'd already received one shock when Godzilla the Dog leaped at me, but little did I know I was about to be hit with a second shock that was even more disturbing. As we sat at the kitchen table, the smile quickly fell from her face and down into her teacup. She sat there, her head bowed, staring blankly at the table top. With very little prompting, Kay began pouring out an all-too-familiar story.

For years, this wife had felt neglected. Her husband gave the best of his week to his thriving business, and she and the children were left with emotional left-overs on the weekends. All the family responsibilities for raising four youngsters fell on her shoulders, and she was exhausted from putting out fires between her husband and the children.

At times she would plead with John to work on their disintegrating relationship, but her cries fell on deaf ears. Too consumed with building up his career, he didn't have time to worry about the way his marriage and family were breaking down.

Kay suffered through the "domestic" neglect that many wives do, but with one added heartache. She was a Christian with a genuine faith, but she knew that when her husband went to church it was more for social contacts, not spiritual growth.

Slowly, as the years went by, his insensitivity had eaten its way to the very core of their relationship—and had begun to poison her heart.

The Ruin of a National Treasure

As I sat with Kay that day, I felt like I was watching the wreck of the Exxon tanker, *Valdez*. Here was a beautiful home and a stunning family. Yet with disharmony and heartache steering at the helm, their family relationships had been guided right onto the rocks, just as that ill-fated oil tanker had been.

Day after day, the poison of a ruptured marriage poured onto their lives, covering the natural beauty of a loving family with three inches of sludge. They had tried to clean up some of the disaster (which their relationship had become), but in many ways the damage was already done. The kids were feeling the tensions at home and beginning to reflect it in their lives, and any interest they might have shown in attending church was now falling dormant.

Kay had been listening to her friends—even to Christian friends—who told her, "Quit being a *doormat,* Kay. You've already gone through too much. *God will forgive you.* Get out of this mess of a marriage, and try again with someone else." She'd even gone to her pastor at the time and to a "Christian" psychologist. Both had told her that *with her husband* she could never hope to get the ship off the rocks—their marriage was dead in the water and unsalvageable.

"I'm not rushing you to leave, and I hadn't planned on telling you any of this," she said to me at the breakfast table, embarrassed by the tears that quickly came to her eyes. "But when the children come home from school today, I'm leaving my husband. We're all moving out. . . . "

I'd like to say that John and Kay's story is unusual, but, unfortunately, it isn't. In working with couples and families for almost two decades, I've seen many such disasters. They have ruined our greatest natural treasure—our families.

From every appearance, a few rags or suction hoses wouldn't begin to repair the damage that had taken place in the Hammers' relationship. In fact, the more I listened, the more I could see why certain "advisors" had told her the landscape of their life would never be the same. From a human standpoint, it certainly did look like the better option might be to pack up and move on than try to rebuild the impossible. But God allowed something miraculous to happen over the next few hours with Kay that transformed her relationship with her husband—and my life as well.

It's been almost fourteen years since that fateful morning at John and Kay's home. And today the Hammers are not only some of our closest friends, but members of our National Board! Their relationship has changed from oil-soaked blackness to a crystal-clear reflection of Christ's love. Even more, their deep friendship and love for each other is a testimony in itself and has turned back many, many couples from the brink of divorce.

Without a clear action plan that points the way to deep waters of intimacy, and avoids the shallow rocks of marital ruin, we're inviting heartache into our homes.

What brought about the change in their lives? That's what this book is all about. The very verses and concepts I first scratched out on a sheet of notebook paper for Kay that day are the same things I've seen God use in the lives of hundreds over the years. I'll be sharing biblical principles that when applied to a relationship—even one washed up and on the rocks—can turn a mess back into a treasure. Learning specific directions for steering clear of danger can also keep a strong marriage or family from running aground. But change only begins at the place we all must start—at the same point the Hammers had to come to.

Planning to Have a Great Marriage and Family?

Whether it's a family, a school, a company, or a sports team, we cannot possibly guide our relationships safely through the waters of our day without a plan. That's the starting point. Without a clear plan of action that points out the way to the deep waters of intimacy and avoids the shallow rocks of marital ruin we're inviting heartache into our homes. It's critical that we clearly plan our lives and not let chance set their course.

There may have been a time in an earlier day when society itself delineated boundaries clearly enough to substitute for a clear purpose at home. But that's simply not true today. We're asking for a natural disaster of our own if we don't have a specific sense of direction for our families. And that's what this book is all about. It's our best effort to give you a workable, biblically based plan of action for building loving, lasting relationships.[1]

Now we know that asking you to adopt a "plan" of action for your home sounds a great deal like work, but we can assure you that the effort spent on steering your relationship into safe waters is far less work than trying to get it off the rocks would be.

Can having a clear plan of action really bring that much change? In one case, taking the time to learn and practice a plan of action turned a group of defeated individuals into an undefeated team:

The Man Who Made History

When our good friend, Norm Evans, was picked by an expansion National Football League team, they were mired in last place. The owner knew a change was needed, so he hired a new head coach. But that was nothing new. He had already hired several coaches, and hadn't changed their fortunes yet. With the way the team was currently playing, this young "upstart" he'd picked would probably be history himself within a year.

As it turned out, this particular coach *would* go into the NFL history books—but not as a failure. Today, even with ups and downs, he has been in the league longer than any other active coach—and there's a reason. He built his men into a champion team by following a clear plan of action.

The year prior to this coach's arrival, the team had a record of three wins and ten losses. Morale was down, motivation was low, and the players' efforts on the field were lack-luster. Norm remembers standing along the sideline with the other players, wondering how they were going to lose each game they played.

Then the new coach arrived in town, and he wasted no time in getting down to business. His first official act was to call a team meeting—and it was one the players would never forget.

He walked into the room, folded his arms, and stood silently in front of them for several minutes. The moments seemed to stretch into hours. He looked from player to player, and from eye to eye. Finally, he spoke in a clear, convincing voice and said, "Men, you're going to be champions of the NFL."

There was an awkward moment of silence in the room. Several of the veterans had to lower their heads to keep their smiles from breaking into laughter. *Sure, coach* . . . they thought. *Anything you say.* . . . But inside they were thinking, *Who's this guy kidding? We've always been losers in this league. Champions? We're not even challengers*! Then the coach laid out the reason he felt certain the team would be successful—a clear plan of action.

"*First,* " he said, "we're going to give you a great game plan each week that works. I'll guarantee that you'll know more about the person you're playing against than anyone except his wife. *Second,* you're going to *practice* that plan until it becomes a natural part of you. *Third,* you're going to *learn the game plan and practice it*—*and win.*"

Bit by bit, the next season saw the wisdom of his strategy unfold. The players learned a specific plan and then practiced it over and over until they felt a confidence in themselves and between each other that they'd never had before. Now they stood on the sidelines wondering how they were going to *win* games— not lose them. In just one short year, they were a different football team. How different?

It was exactly the reverse of the year before; they came out of the blue to win ten games and lose only three. And the next two seasons, the Miami Dolphins, under head coach Don Shula, won the 1972 and 1973 Super Bowls as the best team in pro football.

"That's a great story if you're a football team," you may say, "but the only similarity our marriage has to an NFL team is that we're always taking cheap shots at each other!" Can having a "plan" really make that much of a difference in a marriage relationship—or even with our children? It did for John and Kay.

Kay Hammer didn't know much about the pro football team in nearby Miami when we sat down that morning, but she still had something in common with them. For years, she and John had let circumstances and the emotions of the moment call all the plays in their relationship—and their lives were on the brink of a last place finish as a result. Yet like this pro team, things started to turn around in their lives once they began to follow a clear plan of action and to practice it consistently.

That morning at the Hammers' breakfast table, I scribbled out for her several biblical principles that I was only then beginning to understand and apply in my own home. The scriptural guidelines that broke through that day and gave Kay hope are the very same ones I'll be sharing with you in this book.

A Marriage Mended . . .

By applying these principles, Kay was able to see her marriage turn around in as dramatic a fashion as I've ever witnessed. Her marriage was doomed for the ashheap of divorce, but because of her willingness to follow a biblically based plan, it's alive, active, and growing today. The man she once couldn't wait to get away from is now her best friend . . . and the one with whom she wants to spend the rest of her life.

The secret doesn't just belong to John and Kay—it's available for everyone who desires to have a strong family and a fulfilling marriage. I look forward to the years ahead and get excited about what can happen in families all over this country. I'd love to see hundreds of thousands of husbands, wives, and children make a commitment to do whatever it takes to honor God by following a clear plan for family intimacy. I believe it can happen; in fact, that's the whole goal of our ministry! One of the places you can start is by putting a biblical plan for relationships into action.

To keep our relationships off the rocks, we need to follow two essential steps: we must gain *knowledge* and then *skills* at applying what we've learned. The more we *learn* and *practice* what we've learned, the more gifted we'll become at developing intimate relationships within our homes. In the chapters that follow, we're going to open God's Word and see what He says about making our relationships strong and fulfilling—beginning with the very foundation of a successful family.

Keys to Building Loving, Lasting Relationships

In the next two chapters, we're going to discover that to have any loving and lasting relationship, we must understand:

- *Honor is at the heart of all healthy relationships—and*
- *Genuine love is a decision . . . not a feeling.*

Are you tired of your feelings of love going up and down like a roller coaster? I'll share with you how you can develop a love that remains consistently strong from season to season, year to year. Contrary to popular belief, love is actually a reflection of how much we "honor" another person—for at its core genuine love is a decision, not a feeling.

Second, you'll see that love can best be put into action by mastering and practicing specific skills like:

- *Recognizing the incredible worth of a woman*

I'll spend an entire chapter helping men in particular see how incredibly valuable women are. In particular, we'll see how God seems to have designed within a woman the very talents that can make her an invaluable resource in the home.

- *Learning how to energize our mates in sixty seconds*

One key to loving relationships is the ability to step in when our loved ones are hurting or discouraged. In this section of the book you'll see a method Christ often used with His disciples and others that can help you reach out to those who are facing discouragement, frustration, or a loss of energy.

- *Keeping a major destroyer of relationships out of our homes*

There is a killer lose in many homes today. It can take the life out of a relationship. One thing that I shared with Kay was how to keep the destructive "tapeworm" of anger out of relationships, and how to re-open the spirit of a loved one who may be closed to you.

- *Understanding the tremendous value of a man*

While many couples don't realize it, a man is not a "second class citizen" when it comes to the ability to have strong, lasting relationships. In this section of the book, you'll discover how to tap into a man's God-given gift for nurturing which can form the basis of genuine love. In fact, you'll see in detail four specific skills with which each man comes "naturally" equipped. These can make a tremendous difference in his relationships. *These same four skills are ones a wife must also master to see her relationships deepen and grow as well,* and they include:

- *Providing security to see a marriage bloom and grow*

If a relationship was like a plant, then security would be the sunlight it needs to grow strong and true. In this section, you'll see not only the results of insecurity, but how to build—or re-build—trust and hope in a home.

- *Uncovering a crucial key to meaningful communication*

For everyone who has ever felt misunderstood, there is a way to communicate with our loved ones that provides the greatest understanding—and the least negative reaction. This communication method is used throughout the Scriptures for praise, correction, deeper understanding, and intimacy—and you'll see it strengthen your relationships as well.

- *Keeping courtship alive in your marriage*

Emotional, romantic times can be a constant part of a courtship—and nonexistent in a marriage. In this important aspect of intimacy, you'll see how to keep or regain the elements of courtship, even years after a wedding.

- *Opening the doorway to physical intimacy*

While many people don't realize it, one book of the Bible focuses specifically on the sexual act of marriage—Song of Solomon. Instead of this important area of marital life being a source of frustration, putting some biblical basics into practice can strengthen a couple's physical intimacy, so that this important aspect of married life is no longer a problem.

• *Discovering how to be best friends with your family*

I've spent years studying and personally interviewing "successful" families, and we've consistently found they share one major characteristic. They've all learned the secret of developing family intimacy in even the most difficult of times. We can use that same secret to draw closer to the Lord personally during difficult times as well.

Kay's life did change the day I spoke with her—or at least she had a dramatic change of heart. But her marriage didn't turn around overnight. It took consistent prayer, time, and energy as she began to learn a specific plan of action and how to put it into practice. Even so, the specific skills I laid out to improve her marriage weren't what ultimately made the lasting difference in her life. Those skills made a major impact on her husband, but in themselves they weren't enough to bring the relationship back from the brink of disaster.

Am I saying that her personal force of will and effort to change weren't enough—even when she learned several specific communication and relationship skills? That's exactly right. You see, if we set out, in our flesh or with our own "will power," to guide our relationship into safe waters, I can guarantee that the day will come when we'll fall asleep at the wheel and run aground.[2] If we want to see lasting change in our lives and the lives of our loved ones, we must learn to rely on the only Source able to guard us "day and night."

Without question, the most important section of this book —and of my life—is found in the final two chapters. It is here that Kay Hammer found the power to put into practice all the relationship skills she learned—even when she didn't feel like doing a single one emotionally. For it is only in learning to depend upon the Lord as the Author and Sustainer of any truly successful relationship, that we'll find the inner strength to make lasting changes. And these changes can come—just as they did for John and Kay—by:

• *Learning the art of tapping into the unfailing power source behind a great marriage*

Most of us expect the "gifts" of life—including our spouse and children—to be the "source" of our life and happiness. In this most important section I'll show that while husbands and wives can make great friends and lovers, they make lousy gods. Learning to plug into the only consistent source of love, peace, and joy is the only way to have the spiritual and emotional stamina to withstand the storms of life. And finally, we need to learn how to . . .

- *Turn trials in our homes into lasting benefits for our lives*

"But what if things don't change around here?" "But you never met my husband!" "But you never tried to live with my wife!" "But *your* kids weren't born with a naturally rebellious spirit!"

In every relationship, there are roadblocks that can seem to stand so high they block out any hope of our ever getting past them to intimacy and oneness. And yet in this last section of the book, *you'll see that even the problems we face can do nothing but benefit our lives.* Even more, they can provide a consistent source of deeper love and sensitivity to pass on to others.

Much of the material in this book comes mainly from the "Love Is a Decision" video and film series which, in turn, is based on much of what John Trent and I do in our conferences. It also includes concepts from other books Dr. John Trent and I have done together as well as books I have written individually. Therefore, if you've had the opportunity to read some of the other books we've written, you may recognize some of it as familiar ground. However, in this book's unique format, I've had the opportunity to rewrite and update almost all the major concepts we share at our marriage and relationships seminar. John and I are only able to do eight to ten "Love Is a Decision" seminars a year, but by providing this information for you in this way, I hope it will give you a comprehensive look at what we teach in a way no single book we've done before could ever do.

It's a scary thought that the twenty-first century is right around the corner. And with a new century breathing down our necks, it's unfortunate that most of us don't have a plan for next week, let alone a plan for the next century.

I hope you're different. I hope you'll work at learning and practicing a plan—any plan—that is based on the Scriptures and grounded in His love. If you do use this book as a guideline, it's my prayer that it will be one of the most sensible, down-to-earth books you've ever read. I also hope that once you've read it, you and those you love will never be the same.

I earnestly pray that spending time in these pages will cause you to fall more deeply in love with God and His Word. As a by-product, I hope that loving God and His Word more deeply will then give you practical tools for constructing a mirror image of God's love to reflect to your family. That building process begins in Chapter 2, where we'll discover that all relationships begin with an essential element to a fulfilling life.

2

The Foundation for All Healthy Relationships

It is winter in Washington state, and a cold, wet wind is blowing. Smoke pours from the chimney of a small, two-story white house that looks warm and cozy in the chill night air. In fact, if you were to come close and peek through the kitchen window, you'd see a scene reminiscent of a Norman Rockwell painting.

Inside are a father, a mother, and five children, seated around the kitchen table having dinner. At first glance, it seems to be a portrait of pure Americana. Like the crackling blaze in the nearby fireplace, the scene gives the illusion of emotional warmth. But if you stayed around for a bit, you'd see that looks can be deceiving. For inside is an emotional chill that can cut to the bone like the northern air whistling through the trees.

The American dream starts to disappear when the father reaches over and pops the nearest teenager on the arm with the back of his hand. The teenager fires back a smart remark, and the two begin their nightly yelling match. The rest of the children all join in with a chorus of jeers—some angry, some laughing.

That is, all except the smallest child . . . the young boy sitting across from his father. He sits wide-eyed, his little heart pounding, watching everything that's happening around the table, wondering why his mother looks so sad, and wishing things would be different tonight.

But at this home, it's always this way—the smart remarks, the challenging looks, the unbridled anger. In most homes, there is a soft side and a hard side to life. But for this little boy, there's just one side of life with his father.[1] The cold, rough side that recalls his Dad decking one of his older brothers in anger . . . but never his giving him or his mother a hug.

Before turning away from the window, we see the father jump up from his chair and slap his napkin down on his plate.

"I never get any respect around here!" he shouts. "I'm leaving!"

"Yea, go ahead! *Get outta here!*" the kids shout back, laughing and taunting their father as he stalks out of the room. But for the little boy, it's been another night of conflict and confrontation at the dinner table, and another layer of painful memories to cover his soul . . . memories that are as vivid today as they were almost forty years ago. . . .

I hope this story doesn't bring back personal memories of a hurtful home for you; but it certainly does for me. For that little boy watching wide-eyed at the dinner table, getting all the wrong messages about family relationships, was me.

Over the years, I've thought quite a bit about what happened in my home growing up. Even as a child, I knew something was very wrong. There always seemed to be something missing from our family that kept us intimate strangers—always together but forever apart. For years, however, I had no idea what it was!

Have you ever wondered at times about the missing ingredient in your own relationships? Have you ever been so hurt that you've felt like throwing up your hands in despair? Have you looked at marital or family unity like candy inside a broken gumball machine—taking nickel after nickel after nickel—but never putting intimacy within your grasp?

Join the club. Most of us—even those from very loving homes and happy marriages—have experienced times when our most important relationships were difficult or unfulfilling. Why is it that the intimacy we want so often seems to be just out of reach?

At times, some of us have felt like John and Kay Hammer in Chapter 1—that the answer to all our family's problems is close at hand. Perhaps she's staring us right in the eye, or he's sitting across the table from us or even sleeping next to us at night. If only "that child or spouse" would change and begin meeting some of our expectations, finally our family life could be all it should be!

The Age-Old Mistake

It's easy for us to get excited about *another* person's need to change. For years, I was like a husband I once heard about. In his personal devotions he was reading Proverbs 31, the section in the

Bible that gives a picture of a practically perfect wife. During the course of an average day, this far-from-average woman buys and sells land, feeds the poor, prepares scrumptious meals for the entire household, hand-sews each child's wardrobe, and basically leaps over tall buildings with a single bound.

The more he read about this godly woman, and the more virtues that piled up about her, the more frustrated this husband became with his own wife. Finally, his emotions reaching the boiling point, he picked up his Bible (making sure he kept his finger on the verse to mark his place), and stomped off to find the "source" of all his problems.

Finding her sitting at the kitchen table, he laid the Bible down in front of her and pointed his finger repeatedly at the verses he'd been reading in Proverbs.

"Honey, do you know about this section in the Bible?" It was less a question than a threat.

She glanced nonchalantly at the open Bible in his hand, recognizing the passage.

"Yes," she said, "I know about that section."

After waiting, unrewarded by any further response, he continued, "Look, I know you want to be a godly person, and if you knew about this section. . . ."

Lifting an eyebrow, she repeated more firmly, "Listen—I *know* about that section."

Then straightening up to his full stature, towering over her as she sat at the table, he said, "If you *know* about this section, how come you don't get up every morning and make me a hot meal?"

"Dear," she said, "if you want a hot meal, *light your corn-flakes on fire!*"

By most people's standards this couple might be classified in the "highly strained" category. The story still points up a key problem in many homes. For years I felt that if only my wife Norma would change, every problem in our relationship would disappear. And during all that time, Norma was feeling exactly the same way I was—with one exception. She wanted *me* to change and then marital intimacy would finally be within reach.

But a funny thing happened on our way to changing each other. As much as I pushed Norma to change, and as much as she pulled me, neither one of us ever budged an inch—and neither did our relationship. For many reasons that we'll look at later, when our best efforts go into trying to change another person, we seem to reap the worst relationship rewards.

It's like the wife who noticed the new neighbors who moved in across the street. Every evening, she peeked through the curtains and watched as the husband came home from work.

She couldn't miss the fact that nearly every night, this man would bring home flowers or a little gift for his wife. She'd run to greet him as he got out of the car, and he'd hand her a gift. Then they'd hug and kiss until they had walked inside and closed the door behind them.

> *God's Word contains the only genuine blueprint for successful relationships, both with Him and others.*

One night, after weeks of watching this same gushy scene repeated over and over, the poor neighbor woman finally reached the breaking point. The moment her husband walked in the door, she said, "Have you noticed we have new neighbors across the street?"

As he dropped his briefcase on the floor and fell into the easy chair in front of the television, he replied, "Yeah, I've noticed we have new neighbors."

"But have you noticed what they *do* every night?"

"No, dear," he answered, "I haven't noticed."

She continued, "Every night when he comes home, he gives her a big kiss, he hugs her, and he almost always brings her a special gift." Then she added, "How come *you* don't ever do that?"

Her husband stared at her with a puzzled look on his face and said, "Honey, I can't do that. I hardly know the woman!"

This age-old tactic of trying to get one's mate, friend, child, or boss to change may win a few minor battles, but it never wins the war of unmet expectations. Nonetheless, it was the primary way I tried to improve my marriage for several years.

Looking back now, I deeply regret not having realized how fruitless this approach is. It causes so many more problems than it solves (unhealthy dependency and increased selfishness to name just two). And it forces each marriage partner to be a competitor —not a completer. There have been many times I've wished I could have those years back.

Had I been wiser, Norma and I could have been spared dozens of painful, unnecessary discussions. If only I'd been aware that God had a plan for family relationships—and a personal plan for each one of us—I could have stopped arm-twisting and started arming myself with His wisdom on the family.

The Knowledge and Skills
Necessary for a Great Relationship

God's Word contains the only genuine blueprint for successful relationships, both with Him and with others. Yet, for years, I had been looking at the wrong set of plans. As a husband, I based most of my actions on unhealthy family patterns drawn from my past. Instead, I should have been looking to God's unchanging plan for the family where the results would have been far less frustrating and much more fulfilling.

Over the years, in speaking and counseling with thousands of couples, I've discovered I wasn't alone in coming into marriage without the proper knowledge and skills to nurture a growing relationship. In fact, across our country, the average couple spends more than two hundred hours getting ready for the wedding service, and less than three hours in any type of premarital counseling or preparation.[2]

In every state in our country, it is far easier to get a marriage license than it is to get a driver's license! And yet statistics show time and again that even a small dose of training before marriage can positively affect marital satisfaction and outcome.[3]

In talking with hundreds of couples, I've found that my premarital preparation wasn't far from the norm. It consisted of one meeting with a minister who asked me two questions:

"Gary," he asked, "do you love Norma?"

"Well . . . yes," I said. (Norma was sitting right beside me . . . what else could I say!) But now I realize that I really didn't understand what it meant to truly love her in the way the Scriptures describe.

Then the pastor asked me a second question, "Gary, would you lay down your life for her?"

Again I said yes, thinking he was asking if I would throw myself in front of a truck for her, or step in front of a gunman to take the bullet meant for her.

The truth of the matter is, when I married Norma I knew the right words—but not the right answers. I didn't have a plan to go by, and after marrying a sparky, enthusiastic, godly woman, it took me about five years of applying the wrong information regarding relationships to knock the sparkle right out of her life.

Early in our marriage, I could tell we weren't doing well, so I decided to try a few quick-fix remedies. As I mentioned, I tried the "If you'd just change" tactic, and even resorted to the lecture method of teaching her what the Scriptures say about being a godly wife. I never used an overhead projector, but I probably would have if I'd thought about it. Many a night, 99 percent of my dinner table conversations were actually lectures aimed at drilling into Norma what the Bible said *she* should do to make "us" happy.

During all that time, I conveniently ignored the Scriptural words of wisdom that applied to the husband—probably because I had never taken the time to truly understand the concepts behind the words. And to go one step deeper, without realizing it, I was covering up my own weaknesses and feelings of inadequacy by pointing out hers.

The Death of a Dream . . . the Birth of a Genuine Love

Norma kept hoping that I'd "get with it," but I never did. As she saw her hopes for a warm, fulfilling family life slipping away, she felt resigned to a marriage that would never match her dreams.

After nearly five years of watching our relationship grow more and more strained, I came home one day, walked into the kitchen, and greeted Norma with the usual, "Hi, I'm home." But she didn't respond.

"Is anything wrong?" I asked.

I knew from the look on her face and her nonverbal expressions that I didn't need to ask the question. It was obvious that something was drastically "wrong."

Suddenly, I felt tired all over. I had been battling my conscience for years and spent untold energy to keep up a facade of closeness to those at the church. Here I was teaching and counseling each week on relationships, and in my own marriage I felt like a failure. After years of pretending, I knew I didn't need a quick "self-help" gimmick to get through to my wife. I needed the kind of total heart transplant that only God can give. And so I gently put my arm around her and asked, "Norma, what do *you* think is wrong in our relationship?"

"Oh, no, you don't," Norma said, pulling back from me, her eyes filling with tears.

"You're not going to get me to share what I'm feeling and then turn it into another lecture on what I'm doing wrong."

"Honey," I said, trying to stay as soft as I could, "I can see how you'd feel that way, and I'm very, very sorry, but could you *please* just tell me one more time? I promise you, this time you won't hear a lecture."

Reluctantly, Norma did share with me the concerns that had been building up in her heart, and while it may have been her one hundredth time to tell me, I had never heard it the way she explained it that day. Little did I know that this single conversation would become one of the most traumatic—yet one of the most significant—moments in our lives.

Norma said several important things that afternoon, but there was one thing in particular I'll never forget. I now realize that the problem she explained that day is one of the most common reasons many couples and families struggle for years to find a healthy, meaningful relationship, and yet never quite reach it. She told me:

"Gary, I feel like everything on this earth is far more important to you than I am. . . ."

"I feel that all the football games you watch on television are more important than I am, the newspaper, your hobbies, your counseling at the church. Gary, I can spend hours working in the kitchen, and you never say a word. I can even farm out the kids to a baby-sitter and have a candlelight dinner all prepared for you, and the phone will ring and you'll say, 'Oh, I'm not doing anything important. I'm just eating. Sure, I'll be right over.' Then you're gone, telling me to keep something warm for you in the oven.

"I'm not saying that your counseling isn't important, but many of those couples you talk to have struggled with their problems for *years!* Taking one night out to spend with your wife isn't going to bother them—but it's killing us!

"It's like I don't matter to you, but other people do. In fact, sometimes I feel that you're more polite to total strangers than you are to me. You'll say the most awful things to me, but never to anyone else, especially not people at the church. . . ."

She went on, but you get the point—and so did I. While it may have been a message that was on continuous play around our house, I was hearing the recording loud and clear for the *first* time.

Before talking with Norma, I would never have stood up in front of a group and said that my counseling or even the nonstop sporting events I watched on television were more important than my wife, but without realizing it, that's exactly what I was communicating to her.

Little did I know that for five years of marriage, I had also been violating a crucial biblical concept which lies at the heart of any strong relationship. Every time I ignored its power to build loving, lasting relationships, I was literally shutting the door to the kind of home and family I'd wanted all my life.

What is this biblical principle that I'd been ignoring for years—and that weakened my marriage as a result? It's a simple, yet incredibly powerful, principle, and it comes wrapped in a single word—"honor."[4]

Honor Is the Foundation for All Healthy Relationships

Without a doubt, the concept of honor is the single most important principle we know of for building healthy relationships. It's important for a husband and wife to begin applying it toward each other. And children to apply it toward their parents, and for parents to apply it toward their children. It even works with friend-to-friend relationships. The results of allowing "honor" to reign can be dramatic and life-changing.

Honor is not only the basis of all our earthly relationships, it's at the heart of our relationship with God (see Matthew 6:19–21,

33). Yet we know so little about it that it's almost as if there's an active cover-up going on to keep it a secret from us.[5] To give you an idea of this crucial concept, let's get a brief thumbnail sketch of what "honor" means in the Scriptures.

During biblical times, the word "honor" carried a literal meaning that has been all but lost by translation and time. For a Greek living in Christ's day, something of "honor" called to mind something "heavy, or weighty."[6] Gold, for example, was the perfect picture of something of "honor," because it was heavy and valuable at the same time.

For this same Greek, the word "dishonor" would also bring to mind a literal picture. The word for "dishonor" actually meant "mist" or "steam."[7] Why? Because the lightest, most insignificant thing the Greeks could think of was the steam rising off a pot of boiling water, or clouding a mirror on a cold winter day.

When we honor particular people we're saying in effect that who they are and what they say carries great weight with us. They're extremely valuable in our eyes. Just the opposite is true when we dishonor them. In effect, by our verbal or nonverbal statements we're saying that their words or actions make them of little value or "light-weights" in our eyes.

When the apostle Paul wanted the Corinthian believers to repent from their immoral life-styles and renew their love for Christ, he told them, "You were bought at a price [literally, with "honor"]. Therefore honor God with your body" (1 Corinthians 6:20).

Every angel in heaven and each of us who make up the heavenly hosts of believers will one day sing, "Worthy is the Lamb, who was slain, to receive power . . . wisdom . . . *honor* . . . glory . . . praise" (Revelation 5:12). In both these verses, honoring God means to recognize that nothing on earth or in heaven is as valuable, as weighty, as significant as He.

But how does the concept of honor specifically apply to a marriage relationship?

How to Bring Honor into Your Home

One of the most powerful statements in all the Bible for husbands is, "You husbands, in the same way be considerate as you live with your wives, and treat them with respect (*honor*) as the weaker partner and as heirs with you of the gracious gift of life, so that nothing will hinder your prayers" (1 Peter 3:7).

In 1 Peter 3:1–2 the apostle states the same idea about a wife's relationship with her husband. Do you want to motivate your husband spiritually? Then the apostle says for a wife to use the powerful shaping tool of "honor" by letting him see your genuine and respectful (or honoring) behavior. Finally, a verse that also communicates the mutual need for honor in a home or in any relationship is Romans 12:10. It clearly states, "Be devoted to one another in brotherly love. *Honor* one another above yourselves."

When I came face to face with the concept of "honor" in a home, I suddenly understood why a major part of my prayer life was being hindered. When it came to Norma, the person who from an earthly perspective should receive the "highest value" I could give, I put a hundred things ahead of her. Work projects were more important to me than my mate, and while it's to my shame to admit it, there were countless times that a mountain trout, a small white golf ball, numerous church meetings, close friends and acquaintances—and almost anything "interesting" on television—took the place of honor which should have been reserved for Norma.

If someone had stopped me on the street or at church and asked me if I loved my wife, I would have answered emphatically "Yes!" The problem was, you could never tell I loved Norma by her place of honor (her priority status) in comparison to a hundred more "important" things in my life.

So right there at our kitchen table, I pledged to change. I didn't realize all the implications of what I was doing, but I had a profound sense that things in the Smalley house would never be the same—and they haven't been.

First, I went alone before my Heavenly Father and asked His forgiveness for my incredible selfishness. I realized that at times many things, even good things like my ministry, had taken on more "weight" to me than my relationship with the Lord. That would have to change. I knew that the first step toward giving my wife honor had to be giving God the place of honor reserved only for Him in my life.

It was hard to admit, but I was coming to realize that the idea of honor was out of balance in my life. At that point, something interesting happened. Almost immediately, I noticed it was easier than ever before to pray and read the Scriptures.

Because I valued too many other things of this world more than my time in God's Word, I didn't naturally dive into the Bible and pray early in our marriage. In addition, I wasn't obeying the command of Scripture to give "honor" to my wife. Today, because of my decision to make God the "weightiest" Person in my life—and my commitment to give Norma the "honor" she deserves—one of the most natural things I do in the course of a day is to pray and spend time in His Word. We'll take time to focus on this important issue in a later chapter.

However, while I had come to grips with the concept of honor in my relationship with my Heavenly Father, like Peter, I couldn't stay on the mountaintop. It was time humbly to go back down in the valley to Norma and ask her to forgive me for the way I'd treated her.

"Honey," I said, "I know that we both want to give God first place in our lives. But from an earthly perspective, I want you to be above everything or everyone else in my life."

When Truth Needs a Track Record

Going to Norma was an extremely traumatic moment for me, and it would prove to be a major turning point in my life and in our marriage. But there was one problem. Norma didn't believe me that day.

I knew I had come face to face with the truth of God's Word, and that my life was going to be different as a result, but she just thought it was more empty words. So she threw out a half-convincing, "Yeah, okay," at my vow to honor her and got up from the table to continue preparing dinner.

It's not that Norma lacked faith in God or His Word. From the first time I met her almost twenty-nine years ago until today, I have always been blessed by her deep faith and commitment to Christ. What she lacked wasn't faith in God, but faith in her husband. She needed a track record of being "honored" from a husband who had never practiced it.

I have to admit that at the time, I didn't know exactly what it meant to put the concept of honor into action in our home, but I knew enough to realize that honor would have to be a daily—sometimes hourly—decision. And I had made that decision. I wasn't going to keep Norma on a starvation diet of praise and three full meals of criticism and unrealistic expectations anymore. I was going to consistently feed her with a nourishing meal of significance and high value in our home.

"Norma," I said, "I know you have every reason to doubt me, but I mean what I'm saying. I never understood this before, and I want to ask you to forgive me for making you think that everything else I'm doing is more important than you. No matter how I've acted in the past, that's not what I really believe."

Our evening discussion was over, and she wasn't dazzled by my promise of change. In fact, because of the five years she had lived with the "old Gary," it took her almost two full years of a consistent track record of honoring acts to finally believe the "new Gary" was for real.

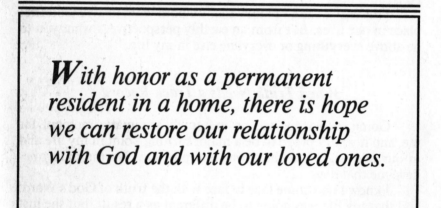

With honor as a permanent resident in a home, there is hope we can restore our relationship with God and with our loved ones.

Norma has never failed to forgive me when I asked her, and she forgave me that day. But she was right to question whether I would actually follow through on my promises. She'd been standing in fifth or sixth place in my life for so long, it was natural for her to be skeptical. It was hard for her to believe she was finally moving to the front of the line.

If you make a decision today to increase the honor in your home, don't be disappointed if your mate doesn't do back-flips until tomorrow or the next month. Remember, he or she has been watching your actions for a long time. They have all your past press clippings cut out and pasted in their memories. And if your previous track record has been less than spectacular—as mine was—emotional scar tissue may cause them to be calloused to your present promises for several months. Hype may sell hamburgers and automobiles, but it doesn't work on your spouse the way time linked with a track record does.

With honor as a permanent resident in a home, there is hope we can restore our relationship with God and with our loved ones. Feelings that have taken years to develop don't change overnight, but persistent honor has the power to win over even the hardest of hearts—particularly as a husband or wife sees affirming actions become a consistent part of a marriage.

Putting Relationships in the Right Order

For me, that fateful conversation with my wife at the kitchen table forced me to get my spiritual and family life in order. In fact, I actually began to prioritize my life from zero to ten, zero being something of little value, ten something of highest value.

I established God and my relationship with Christ as the highest—a ten. On a consistent basis, I began looking at my spiritual life and asking the question, "One to ten, where is my spiritual life with Christ?" "How highly do I value His Word?" "Prayer?" "Sharing my faith?"

Then I placed Norma above everything else on this earth, way up in the nines. With this relationship, too, I often asked myself (and Norma), "How am I doing at making you feel like you're up in the high nines, above every one of my hobbies and friends and favorite sports teams? What can I do to keep you believing you're a high nine?"

How about you? If you were to rate the "honor" quotient of your marriage relationship right now, where would it be? Where do you think your spouse would rate it? Have you asked him or her lately?

You're probably as convinced as I am that we need to give God the honor He deserves first, and then make honor a nonnegotiable item in our home, but you may still have questions about how to honor those you love in a practical way.

Let's bring honor out of the cloudland of theory right down to the cobblestone level where we live. Let me share with you three ways to bring honor off the pages of Scripture and right into your home. Each has been life-tested in my home and in the lives of thousands of people at our seminars. It all begins with practicing the "ah-h-h-h-h-h" principle on a regular basis.

Three Ways to Honor Your Loved Ones

1. The "Ah-h-h-h-h-h" Principle

As I've noted, the most fulfilling relationships in life begin with honor. In fact, the Bible says that the "fear" of the Lord—the honor and respect we give Him—is the beginning of wisdom.

The fear of the Lord is being "awe-inspired." For Moses it happened as he beheld the burning bush (Exodus 3). For Elijah the Prophet it came as he listened for the still, small voice as God's glory paraded by (1 Kings 19). And for Peter the fisherman, it was the result of watching Christ calm a rolling sea with only three words (Mark 4:39). In each case, being in God's presence produced reverence and "awe."

In fact, the fear of the Lord is being so awed that you drop your jaw and inhale a gasp, catching your breath in an audible "ah-h-h-h-h-h." It's a gasp of reverence mixed with a bit of wonder.

In short, honor is a reflex of the heart toward one who is deeply treasured. It's the conviction that you are in the presence of somebody so valuable it's "ah-h-h-h-inspiring." It's important to realize too that this life-changing attitude doesn't start with a feeling—it's a *decision;* and the *feelings* of "awe" eventually follow.

Picture it this way. Let's say you're a homemaker who has taken a well-deserved winter break from housework. It's spring now, and you've decided to pull the house back in order.

You reach into the pantry and take out a can of Johnson's Wax and begin to clean the parquet floor. You've been working an entire twenty minutes when the doorbell rings. Since you were just getting ready to take a break anyway, you cheerfully get up off the floor you've been scrubbing and head to the door.

As it opens and you look up, there stands the President of the United States in the flesh, flanked by two husky Secret Service guards.

"Hi," the president says. "I was just walking in the neighborhood and thought I'd stop in and ask you a few of your thoughts on my foreign policy."

As you stand there with your wet sponge dripping on your

fuzzy slippers, how do you respond? Can you picture the president suddenly showing up at your door to ask a question? No matter what your political viewpoint, having the main occupant of the White House suddenly appear at your doorstep would be cause for a breath-catching gasp of reverence mixed with awe—the "Ah-h-h-h-h-h" response.

Now, I agree that having the president show up at your home for a foreign policy discussion is far fetched, but every day, we see examples of the "Ah-h-h-h-h-h" principle at work. If you've ever been called to jury duty, what does the bailiff say as the judge enters the courtroom?

"Would everyone please rise? The Ah-h-h-h-honorable Judge Wapner is entering the room." It's time to stand up and show ah-h-h-h-honor because someone extremely valuable is about to enter the room.

What do the Orientals do upon meeting someone important or upon signing an important agreement? They bow to each other as a symbol of honor. The gesture means that I have decided you're important and deserve special merit and respect.

Sometimes I walk in the house and see one of my kids sitting in the easy chair watching television. Just for fun, I'll drop to my knees and say, "Unbelieeeevable! I'm actually in the same room with Michael Smalley! I can't believe that I'm living in the same house with somebody as ah-h-h-h-h-mazing as you!"

My kids usually howl, "Da-a-ad." But basically, that is the way you build the "Ah-h-h-h" principle into your relationship. You decide that the people around you—your spouse, your children, your friends, and your parents—are worthy of honor. They are worth an "ah-h-h-h-h-h" on a consistent basis.

Have you ever wondered why the dog is considered man's best friend? As you'll discover in Chapter 5, it's because men, in particular, are extremely motivated by the "Ah-h-h-h-h-h" principle.[8]

Think about the way the average dog greets its owner. Whether you've been gone for two weeks on vacation or ten minutes to the mini-mart, he probably falls all over himself showing his happiness at seeing you. Nonverbally, dogs honor their owners with massive doses of love and enthusiasm. In fact, I'm sure that if the dog could gasp, "ah-h-h-h-h!" when he saw you walk in, he would!

That's probably one reason why men tend to dislike cats. You can call them and they just give you that "Garfield" look of disdain, as if they were saying, "Where do you get off thinking you're valuable enough for me to come running over to you? *I'm the one who gets honored around here!*"

In the book of Proverbs, we're told that even the smallest act of "ah-h-h-h-h" can have a positive effect on a relationship. There we read, "Bright eyes gladden the heart . . ." (Proverbs 15:30, NASB).

Have you ever appeared at a surprise party for a special friend and seen their eyes "light up" when they see you? That same feeling of "I'm really special to them" is at the heart of having "bright eyes." And where do "bright eyes" come from? From a heart that is looking at someone very, very special to us—someone we're delighted to see. Someone we're ah-h-h-h-honoring.

2. Remember That "Ah-h-h-h-h-h" Is in the Eye of the Beholder

When we honor someone, we make a decision that a person is special and important. Biblically (and thankfully), honor was not always something that had to be earned. It was given as an act of grace to someone who didn't deserve it.

An example of this is the verse, "While we were still sinners, Christ died for us" (Romans 5:8). Just like our Lord, we sometimes need to make our decision to honor someone apart from our feelings about that person.

It's amazing how a person's response to something or someone can change dramatically once they've made a decision that the individual is truly valuable. That fact was never more clear to me than after what happened at a special seminar we did that was filmed for a nationwide television audience.

Jim Shaughnessy is a close friend who has been to several of our "Love Is a Decision" Seminars, and he knows that I always teach a section on honoring those we love. Without me knowing it, he planned something for this special seminar that brought about the greatest natural "Ah-h-h-h-h-h" response from a crowd I've ever witnessed.

At most of our seminars, I use a three-inch piece of sparkling crystal cut in the shape of a diamond to give people a word picture of "honor." I usually begin by asking the audience:

"How many of you believe this cut stone is a $100,000 diamond?" A chuckle will ripple through the audience as people look at the crystal. Usually, I have to talk at least one person into raising his hand just so I can continue with the point I'm making.

Truthfully, people should chuckle when they hear me put the value of that piece of crystal at $100,000. After all, it's probably not worth more than sixty dollars in any store in the country, but as far as I'm concerned I wouldn't part with it for one penny less than $100,000.

It's kind of like the farmer who crossed fifty pigs with fifty deer—and got a hundred sows and bucks! *It's we who set the value of something.* And that was a fact my friend helped me illustrate better than I could have ever dreamed.

Jim owns a very old Stradivarius violin. Just for the television special, he had it flown in—complete with its own "security guard"! As I began to talk about honor in the seminar, I brought out what looked just like any old, unstrung fiddle or violin.

"This violin is worth over $65,000," I said. I could see by the smiles and nodding of heads that people believed me about as much as they did when I would hold up my "$100,000" diamond. In fact, my holding up the violin didn't produce even one "ah-h-h-h-hdible" gasp in the entire crowd. After all, they could see with their own eyes that it was an old violin. Particularly those sitting close to the speaker's platform could see that it didn't even have any strings.

But as I talked about attaching honor to something, I told them a little bit more about what I actually held in my hand. After all, there are only about 600 violins like it left in the world, and when I angled it so that I could read the inscription inside, and then mentioned the word "Stradivarius," the effect was incredible.

A spontaneous, collective, breath-catching "ah-h-h-h" reflex rifled throughout the crowd. Just a few moments before, it was just an old violin, not worthy of any special honor, but by attaching that one word, "Stradivarius," to it, it suddenly was given a high place of honor by everyone in the room (especially by me as I hoped I wouldn't drop it!).

Remember, people make the decision that something is of high value. Does a Chevy pull up to a Mercedes at a stoplight and gaze at it enviously, wishing it could be a Mercedes? Of course not. Do you think that silver cries itself to sleep each night because it's not as valuable as gold? It doesn't care. *We're* the ones that attach value to a thing—or a person.

Someone came up with a great idea years ago. They decided to take all the old pieces of furniture sitting around in people's attics and garages and call them "antiques." Instantly, people lined up to pay exorbitant prices for all these old pieces of "junk." Then, after spending huge amounts that would make new furniture prices blush, they take home these worn relics and spend countless hours and extra dollars refinishing them!

What happened to all those old sticks of furniture to make them suddenly become antiques? Their value suddenly rose, and that happened for only one reason—we had decided they were more valuable to us. I was aware of this concept everywhere else in life, but I wasn't practicing it in my own home—the most important place for the "Ah-h-h-h-h-h" principle to take root and grow.

Let's say the husband comes home at night and the whole family meets him at the door. Instead of running past him to go out to play or to watch television, he is greeted with a collective chorus of "*Ah-h-h-h-h! Look who's here!!*"

Then, to his amazement, the wife and kids roll out a red carpet runner into the house and as he walks down it, the kids throw rose petals at his feet. Scurrying ahead of him, they usher him into his easy chair, prop up his feet, lovingly hand him his paper, and peel grapes for him, throwing them (at an angle) into his mouth to eat.

What would the average husband think if he was greeted this way when he walked in the door? He'd probably think he was in the wrong house! Honoring actions don't have to be exaggerated the way I've described above. But the attitude of honor does have to be present if our relationships are to grow and develop.

"Hold it," I can hear someone saying, "what if some people don't *deserve* our honor? How can I act in an honoring way toward them when they're not living up to what I want?"

Whether it is a husband or a wife who asks that question about the person they vowed to honor, it takes another question to answer it: Do you want your relationship to blossom instead of wither? If the answer is "blossom," then you can't avoid the issue of honor in a home.

You may be concerned that honoring an undeserving mate will make things worse rather than better. Or you may even be worried your mate will take advantage of you and use you because of your willingness to treat them with respect. However, before you react to what I'm saying and close the book, please try to understand how love and honor intermingle.

I know that God is the only being in life who is always worthy of honor, and yet in His Word we are told to honor others —all others. Children are to give "honor" to their parents. A husband should honor his wife and a wife her husband. We are to prefer "one another" in honor.

Remember, honor is an *attitude* that someone is valuable.

It is not an absolution of all a person's faults, nor a command to be less than honest with who they are. Let me give you an example:

I have a good friend whose father is an alcoholic. I know for a fact that this man "honors" his father by praying for him, encouraging him to accept Christ, and even inviting him to his home consistently.

But "honor" does not mean that he allows his alcoholic father to drive his three-year-old daughter around in his car. Neither does honor dissolve all healthy boundaries in their relationship. There is no swearing allowed, no smoking in the house, and no "teasing" the children. There are times when the father doesn't want to play by the rules—and doesn't come to the house as a result. But he knows and has even admitted—in spite of his complaints—that his son "honors" and even loves him.

"Honor" doesn't cast pearls before swine—but neither does it mean that you treat a person like a swine until he measures up to your standards.

If you're in the situation of having to "honor" a difficult person, you may want to go deeper into several books that John Trent and I have written on this subject and can also recommend.[9] Without exception, be sure to read and absorb everything I cover in Chapters 13 and 14 in this book.

The material in these chapters (on tapping into the very power source of love) will be especially helpful for you. There you will find the secret to really enjoying life in spite of difficult circumstances. The concepts found there are also absolutely crucial for working through the fear of "What if they won't change?"

There have been times when I have been motivated to honor Norma not out of my "feelings," but as an act of my will and in obedience to God's command that I do so. And consistently, once I put honor in its right place, positive, loving feelings will follow.

Is this some type of psychological trick or basis for manipulation? Hardly. It's actually a biblical principle:

In Matthew 6:21 Jesus said, ". . . for where your treasure is, there your heart will be also." In other words, when it comes to our spiritual life, what we treasure—what we place high value upon—is where our feelings reside. The same thing is true in my relationship with my spouse. If I "treasure" or honor a person, my positive, warm feelings about him or her begin to rise correspondingly.

I realize that it isn't always easy to keep one's thoughts and feelings at the "honoring" level. As a wife, you might begin to grumble about the little things your husband does that irritate you. There's the trash can that only gets taken out when you remind him for the tenth time, or the way he remembers to fill up *his* car but always forgets to check out yours. As a husband, you may be frustrated with her weight or her discipline of the children or even with the way she drives at night.

But if an attitude of dishonor is allowed to develop or turn destructive, it's a short step to attaching negative feeling to that *person,* instead of his actions. When men (or women) begin a pattern of consistently dishonoring their spouses—even if it's only in their minds—within a matter of a few weeks they can lose nearly all their loving feelings for them.

That's when you begin to hear the comments, "Why did I pick this guy?" or "Of all the fish in the sea, I got stuck with her!" That's also where small acts of irritation—like squeezing the toothpaste tube from the wrong end—can end up being "grounds" for divorce.

But the opposite is true as well. Time and again, when honor begins to take root in a home, within a matter of a few days or weeks, your feelings will start to change. Your husband may seem like a beat-up old violin, but the moment you begin treating him like a Stradivarius, your world and his can change for the better.

There is a third way to keep honor inside your home. We must concentrate on keeping dishonoring acts—even minor ones —outside of our experience.

3. It's Worth the Hard Work to Keep Dishonoring Actions at Arm's Length

It takes time for honor to take root in our lives, and before it does, all of us are capable of the type of thing I used to do. It violated this crucial principle.

As is typical of all small children, every now and then they need a little "motivation" to behave. Ours were no exception. When the need arose for discipline, I'd often take my thumb and middle finger and "flick" them on the head.

"Greg," I'd say, and flick him on the head, "turn off the television!" or "Michael," flick, "stop bothering the dog."

One night we were in a restaurant, and the kids were acting up. As usual, I reached across the table and flicked my daughter on the head to get her to stop pestering her brother.

"*Gary,*" Norma said, in an icy tone, "we're in a restaurant. Is this any kind of place to flick your daughter?"

Her reaction startled me. After all, flicking my kids had become such a habit, I never stopped to think it was dishonoring, so I turned to my daughter and asked, "Kari, how does it make you feel when I flick you?"

"Daddy, I don't like you flicking me." Without an invitation to comment, my two boys quickly agreed.

"Yeah, Dad. We don't like you flicking us *either.*" Norma didn't say anything at this point because I had never flicked her.

Right there I decided to quit flicking the kids, but I knew that since it was a habit, I'd need some incentive to remind me not to dishonor them. So, after thinking about it for a minute, I said, "I'll tell you what, kids. I don't want to dishonor you any more by flicking you. Will you forgive me?" They nodded their heads.

"To show you how serious I am about wanting to stop, I'll make a deal with you. From now on, anytime I flick you I'll give you a dollar right on the spot."

Their immediate response after looking at each other, was, "Flick on, Dad, flick on!"

Let's start making a mental list of what we do that can dishonor our family or friends. Here's our current list of the top ten dishonoring acts we have reported to us all over the country. They're not in a particular "dishonoring" order, but all of them can be killers of meaningful relationships.

The Top Ten Dishonoring Acts in a Home

- Ignoring or degrading another person's opinions, advice, or beliefs (especially criticizing another person's faith)
- Burying oneself in the television or newspaper when another person is trying to communicate with us
- Creating jokes about another person's weak areas or shortcomings (Sarcasm or cutting jokes act like powerful emotional word pictures and do lasting harm in a relationship.)[10]

- Making regular verbal attacks on loved ones: criticizing harshly, being judgmental, delivering uncaring lectures
- Treating in-laws or other relatives as unimportant in one's planning and communication
- Ignoring or simply not expressing appreciation for kind deeds done for us
- Distasteful habits that are practiced in front of the family —even after we are asked to stop
- Overcommiting ourselves to other projects or people so that everything outside the home seems more important than those inside the home
- Power struggles that leave one person feeling that he or she is a child or is being harshly dominated
- An unwillingness to admit that we are wrong or ask forgiveness

I don't want my wife or children to feel any less loved than God would have them be in my home, and that means that honor must become an everyday activity in my life—like shaving or taking time out for meals. How about you? Are you ready to turn loose the "Ah-h-h-h-h-h" Principle in your home?

In this chapter, we've talked about the decision we all need to make to honor others—that people are worth our time and energy! Now, in the next chapter, let's look at the second greatest aspect of any healthy relationship: love. *You'll discover that love is the action we take to communicate how valuable another is* and, like honor, that love is actually a *decision.*

3

Love Is a Decision

Imagine that you've pulled up a chair next to me as I sit facing Kay Hammer, the woman whose story began this book. Like me, you can sense the tension around the table as it soon becomes obvious that the only thing standing between her and the door are the words that will be shared during the next few hours.

What do you say to a woman who was clinging to the end of her rope when it came to her willingness to hang on to her marriage? As you sit with me, you'd hear me tell her that she should try once more to hold her marriage together, but you'd also hear reason after reason why she should leave John. You would hear me tell her how important it is that God be given every opportunity to keep them together—and sharing the latest research that shows the life-long emotional pain that children and spouses suffer after divorce.[1]

Kay listened and agreed to stay with John after our conversation. But I never realized that things were about to get much worse for her and her husband, not better. In fact, he did something a few weeks later that even caused her Christian friends to say to her, "Kay, *leave* him. You shouldn't take that from anybody. . . ."

At first it took an hourly decision to stay, but with each day, Kay became more committed to do what we share in Chapter 13 and especially Chapter 14. She made a decision to respond to her husband out of the fullness of her love for Christ—not the empty feelings she had about her marriage. And the difference in her attitude instantly began to show. But a severe test was coming of how much Kay was willing to seek God's love first, and then reflect it back to her husband. For a few weeks later, he ripped away the most important thing to her in a moment's notice.

Almost Too Much to Take

John couldn't help but notice the change that had come over his wife. Like many mates who see the first blush of change—he tested her to see how real it was.

For two years, Kay's life-line of support had been her Bible Study Fellowship group. These ladies had prayed for her and encouraged her on those hopeless mornings when she was ready to toss in the towel. As a group leader, the highlight of Kay's year was the annual "leaders' retreat" coming up.

She had already paid her money and arranged for babysitting for the children. Kay was less than twenty-four hours away from heading to the airport and the retreat when John came home from the office.

"Where are *you* going?" he demanded, looking around at the suitcases she'd packed.

"To the Bible study leaders' retreat," Kay said. "You know that I leave tomorrow."

"Well, I've changed my mind," John announced. "I don't want you to go. In fact, I think you're spending way too much time with this group. I want you out of that leadership program right now."

Can you imagine the choice she had to make? To stand against her husband and go to the retreat would be to play the same chorus of "I'll do it *my* way" that she had sung unsuccessfully for years. On the other hand, to follow his leadership—and cut herself off from her primary source of fellowship and spiritual support—seemed equally wrong.

What was she to do? This wasn't a situation where she could change the channel and have her decision go away. She could tell John was waiting for her response. What's more, she knew that this was a major test of her "decision" to show him honor, no matter what the circumstances. Just then the phone rang, and she was saved from having to respond to him on the spot.

It was a friend calling to ask if she and John could come to dinner that night with a noted pastor who was speaking in town—a man named Ray Stedman. John and Kay ended up going to the dinner, and as soon as she could, Kay drew Dr. Stedman aside and explained her situation.

"What should I do?" she asked. "What can I say to my husband that will get him to change his mind about my going to the retreat and being in leadership?"

Kay would never forget what this wise pastor told her:

"Kay," he said, "your first responsibility is to seek the Lord, then your family, and *then* a ministry. I'm not going to talk to you about a way to manipulate John to change his mind. If your husband tells you to get out of Bible Study Fellowship, then when I leave tonight you tell him that you're getting out!"

At the time, she thought someone had tossed four gallons of ice water right in her face. She sat with her mouth open wondering, *How could he say such a thing?* Yet as the evening wore on, she realized that what he said was right. For years, she had tried with varying degrees of success to manipulate her way in and out of things—and now she was being asked to change. It was like hearing an army trumpet sound general quarters. The pastor's words called out that she was in the midst of a spiritual battle—not just a battle with her husband.

When they got home from dinner, Kay's normal response would have been, "There is not enough money in this *world* that could keep me home from this retreat. We already agreed that I could go, and you're breaking that promise!"

But instead, her response was based on a decision that God was in control of her life. "If John doesn't want me to go," she said, "then God must not want me to go this time."

"Father," she prayed, "I don't understand why, but I feel like this is a test. So, Lord, please help me find a reason for my not going."

As she looked at her plane tickets lying on the piano, tears filled her eyes. Yet, in spite of the pain, with all her heart she knew what she was doing was right. It was one of the most difficult things she'd ever done in her life, but she walked up the stairs and told her husband that she would skip the retreat, that she would drop out of her leadership position.

We live in days and times where words like "sacrifice" and "commitment" are four-letter words. I realize that, to many people, Kay's decision to love and honor her husband's wishes might seem unenlightened or even terribly wrong. After all, *she had her rights.* But as Kay was to find out, it was in laying down her rights that she finally broke through to her husband.

In simple terms what Kay literally did was make love a decision. *Genuine love is honor put into action regardless of the cost.* It comes from a heart overflowing with love for God, freeing us to seek another person's best interests. Kay knew that only by loving God first and foremost could she ever hope to pull off loving John

—especially after what he had done. Every "instinct" she had told her to lash out. Yet in spite of her "instincts," her love would be based on a decision to honor her husband—not her emotions.

Let me admit that there are situations where either the husband or wife is emotionally unhealthy. In no way am I saying that we are to give a "blanket" yes to a spouse who commands us to do something against the law or in direct violation to God's law. (For a look at the balance between unconditional love and dealing with an emotionally destructive person, we recommend Dr. James Dobson's *Love Must Be Tough*). But Kay believed this was her chance to prove to John what was more important: her husband or her retreat. Perhaps that's why she determined more than ever that her love for Christ would be the basis of her love for her husband. And that's what led to . . . the rest of the story.

The Rest of the Story

Several months passed, and John and Kay were invited to a large Christian conference held in the auditorium at Indiana University. At the conclusion of the seminar, the speaker did something unusual. He opened up several microphones for people in the audience to come up and share what God had been doing in their lives. That's when it happened.

Kay suddenly looked over and noticed that John was getting up from his seat and heading to the front of the auditorium. He waited his turn in line and then stepped up to the microphone.

"Ladies and gentlemen," he said to a group of over a thousand people. "*I just want you to know that I'm here tonight because my wife First Peter three'ed me into coming!*"

The entire place came unglued with laughter as his words sank in. Indeed, as the verse says, Kay's commitment to trust God had won over her husband "without a word" by her godly actions (1 Peter 3:1–6).

"I'm going to tell you all something Kay doesn't know," John continued. "We had this guy named Gary Smalley come to our house and I don't know what he told my wife—but things haven't been the same since. Basically, I'm here tonight because my wife has worn me out with her love.

"I've got to confess that there have been days when I actually sat in my office, thinking up something I was going to tell her to do when I got home *just to see if she would do it*—and she did!

Watching the reality of this woman's love for God is the reason I'm standing up here tonight. . . ." And there was more to come.

John changed so much that soon *he* was in the leadership program of the *Men's* Bible Study Fellowship. And then came the day of *their* men's leadership retreat. Kay drove her husband to where the bus would take him and several others on a weekend retreat. John had never been on a men's retreat, and he was like a schoolboy going to summer camp for the first time.

> *Genuine love is honor put into action regardless of the cost.*

While she never said anything at the bus station, Kay couldn't help thinking about the retreat she had given up months earlier. And as she drove off, the emotions of the moment finally hit her. She was thankful for the changes in her husband's life, but the hurt of being denied an opportunity to go to her own leaders' retreat brought tears to her eyes—until the phone rang.

Kay had barely gotten back home when John called.

"We're at a truck stop picking up some other people for the retreat," he said, "and I just had to call you."

With his voice choking with emotion, he said, "Kay, I've been thinking back to a time I told you you couldn't go to a retreat. Could you forgive me for asking you to give up something I knew was really important to you? I'm so sorry I asked you to step down from your leadership group. I never should have asked what I did, and I never will again. Can you find it in your heart to forgive me? . . ."

Kay has been to many retreats since the one she missed over thirteen years ago—but none have held as much meaning as the one she never attended. Later, she would say in reflecting on that unforgettable call, "*I gave up a retreat—but I gained back a husband!*"

Over the years, John and Kay have developed a rock-solid love for Christ and each other. This couple whose relationship at one time was dead in the water, held fast by the rocks of insensitivity and bitter arguments, now help countless couples fight back from the brink of divorce. And they do this by sharing the reality of their own story—and by helping others see that genuine love is a decision, not a feeling.

Moving Honor into a Home by Loving Actions

I realize that there are times when love needs to be tough and set firm boundaries with a loved one. But what turned around John and Kay's life was a principle that is true in any home. *The most effective way to open the door to needed changes in a relationship is to honor a loved one. And once we've made that decision to honor, love is the action we take no matter how we feel.*

Genuine love is honor put into action, regardless of the cost. It comes from a heart overflowing with affection for God, freeing us to seek another person's best interest.

In a nutshell, that definition is an outline of this book. We've already seen in Chapter 2 that honor is at the foundation of all healthy relationships. Now we've seen that out of our decision to honor flows loving actions *regardless of our feelings—regardless of the cost.*

Now in the chapters that follow, you'll learn the ten areas that took me all day to teach Kay, and that I've spent fifteen years refining and researching ever since. Each one is a *specific loving action* that expresses the honor and the decision to love that we've made.

The very first loving action that is so essential in any home or relationship is recognizing the incredible worth of a woman. Every woman has two tremendous tendencies that we'll uncover for you. What's more, you'll see that there are three questions any husband can ask his wife that can reveal her built-in marriage manual.

4

The Incredible Worth of a Woman

One of the greatest joys I have in teaching the "Love Is a Decision" Seminar is sharing with men how incredibly valuable women are. Why? One major reason is that I've spent time learning and asking questions from women. That includes twenty-five years of marriage, and interviewing over 30,000 women at conferences and in counseling sessions across the country. I've seen, first hand, the tremendous relationship skills that God has woven into the fabric of their lives.

But a few years ago, I had an experience that gave me a whole new appreciation for their incredible worth. For on a windblown afternoon, one woman's "intuitive" senses quite possibly saved my life, and the lives of several others as well.

A River Gone Wild. . . .

It was mid-May, and time for our annual "staff retreat" where we do more retreating than staffing. We did have one legitimate reason for spending the weekend fishing. We were in the process of interviewing Steve Lyon, now an invaluable associate on our staff, and we decided that spending a weekend quizzing him at our favorite fishing spot was just the place to get to know him—and a few trophy-sized trout at the same time.

We were on our way to Lee's Ferry, located just below Lake Powell on the Colorado River. Lying at the mouth of the Grand Canyon, it offers great fishing and some of the most spectacular scenery in the world.

Early the first morning, we waited at the dock for our two guides. Soon, a truck rumbled up, two figures bouncing in the front seat as it rolled to a stop. The door opened and out stepped a tall, weather-beaten man of about forty. Beside him was his wife, a petite woman only half his size. What I would discover later that day was that anything she lacked in size, she would more than make up for in fishing skill—and her natural female "instincts."

Beautiful canyon walls rose literally two and three hundred feet straight up from the edge of the water as we began a tour of the Grand Canyon at water level. It took our boats nearly an hour traveling upstream to reach the dam which stood as a towering marker to "the end of the line." We shut our engines down and quietly began to drift with the current, letting out line behind us as we trolled for speckled and rainbow trout.

The early morning passed with little success. Then lunch time rolled around and we beached the boats about halfway back to the dock. It had been a fairly calm morning, but by the time we got back to the boats, the wind had changed from a whisper to a stiff breeze. I remember thinking, *We won't catch a thing until these gusts die down.* But they didn't.

With each passing minute, the wind grew stronger and more steady. The once glassy surface of the river was beginning to roll as the water churned with a thousand tiny waves. But we were all seasoned campers and fishermen. *What's a little wind?* I thought.

As we got back in the boats, I noticed our two guides talking. I couldn't hear the words they were saying, but it was obvious they were in the midst of a heated discussion. Finally, the man shrugged his shoulders, nodded his head, and marched over to us with some unwelcome news.

"I'm sorry, guys, but we're going to have to pack it in for right now. I can't explain it, but my wife really feels strongly that this isn't just a minor front coming in—and I've learned to listen to her on these waters. So we're heading back."

It was a good thing we listened to her when we did. Almost instantly the wind began to howl, and the waves were beginning to form whitecaps. Within minutes, we lost the ability to communicate from boat to boat as the fury of a desert windstorm drowned out even the most desperate attempts to shout instructions.

We were all on our own to make it back. By now the wind was blowing with such a galelike force that if we had turned sideways to the current, we would have easily been swamped by the angry swells. The only hope we had of making it back on top of the water was to point the boats directly downstream into the wind, meet the waves head on, and speed full throttle to dock and safety.

For thirty minutes (they seemed like a life-time), our three boats fought a river gone wild. A major storm had turned the narrow Canyon walls into a wind-tunnel. I had no idea at the time what was going on in the other two boats, but I knew that prayer kept ours afloat.

Finally, after stopping to bail out water at one point, all three boats had docked safely with all hands accounted for. I learned later from my two sons, who were in the guide's wife's boat, that she had handled herself beautifully. In fact, she was the first one back to the dock. At one point, a gust of wind caught the front end of the boat and began to flip it over backwards, but her cool-headed reaction, at the very least, saved everyone from an icy swim. At most, she saved my sons' lives.

I walked away from that trip with another reason why women are so incredibly valuable. I know for a fact that if our guide hadn't listened to his wife, we would have been in major trouble.

It's struck me several times since that incident how much I've profited from learning the valuable character traits and natural talents that God has built into my wife. Far from an attempt to erase all differences between the sexes, I feel strongly that God placed the differences there for a purpose.

In this chapter, we'll look at several areas of natural, complementing strengths in men and women. I hope one result for every man will be that he finds new reasons for treasuring and valuing his wife, and I hope that one result for every woman will be to find yet another reason to thank God for the natural gifts she brings to those she loves.

Meeting Our Missing Part

It was a wise and loving God who said, "It is not good for the man to be alone" (Genesis 2:18a). But was a woman designed merely to provide a man with companionship—or does it go deeper than that?

Most people are familiar with the passage that talks about God creating woman and His words, "I will make (him, Adam) a helper suitable for him" (Genesis 2:18b). The Hebrew word for "helper" actually means "completer." The word is used throughout the Old Testament to talk about God being our "helper," the One who "completes what is lacking," or "does for us what we cannot do for ourselves."[1]

One of the things that should increase the "honor" a husband gives to his wife is realizing that God created her to help him in areas he isn't naturally equipped to handle. In other words, a wife is designed to bring strengths to the relationship that the husband does not naturally have himself.

Over the years, I've noted a number of ways in which men and women are different, but there are four areas in particular, I've seen a woman's natural gifts act like missing parts needed to complete a man. That first missing piece comes with a special language that a woman speaks which cannot only strengthen a marriage—it can literally be a life-saving gift to some husbands.

1. Two Languages in the Same Home

One study of little four-year-old boys and girls recorded every noise that came out of their mouths over a period of time.[2] The study concluded that 100 percent of the sounds made by little girls had something to do with literal words. They spent a great deal of time talking to each other, and almost an equal amount of time talking to themselves.

For little boys, however, the figure was only 60 percent words. The remaining 40 percent were simply noises and sound effects (like Bzzzzzzzz!, Zooooooooom! Baaammmmmm!). In short, the tendency in even little girls is to use more words than little boys, and that early difference in language skills holds up throughout each age level.

Not only are women more verbal, but they often speak a different language than men do. I'm not talking about homes where English and Spanish, or Japanese and English are spoken, but about a much more common family environment where "Womaneise" and "Maneise" are spoken!

In roughly 80 percent of all homes, men primarily relate to their wives using what we call a *language of the head* while women tend to speak a *language of the heart*.

Typically, men tend to be logical, factual, and detail-oriented. In general, when a man runs out of facts to talk about in a conversation, he often stops talking! Usually, men don't have as much of a need to share as deeply or consistently as do their wives. Nor do they have the need to speak the same number of words their wives do. Some studies have shown that the average woman speaks roughly 25,000 words a day, while the average man speaks only 12,500! What this can mean in a marriage is that a woman is often left holding her cup out for meaningful conversation day after day and drawing it back with only a few drops to nourish her.

On the other hand, women often speak a *language of the heart.* In most cases, they love to share thoughts, feelings, goals, and dreams. A woman's natural skills at communicating often will make her wonderfully sensitive to small things others are thinking, saying, or feeling. And her desire for deep relationships usually exceeds what the average man desires.

It's almost as if men are two-humped camels. They can take a little conversation and then go for days across even the most difficult terrain without any need for more "watering" words, but a woman covering the same distances needs a daily allotment of water to survive and flourish—and often double that ration of "watering" words during difficult periods in her life.

Why should a man be interested in having his wife help him learn to speak her "language of the heart"? For one thing, it can actually help him live longer.

In his provocative book, *The Language of the Heart,* Dr. James J. Lynch presents compelling evidence that effective communication skills can do wonders for a person's cardiovascular health.[3] Whether we realize it or not, each time we engage in conversation, whether we are under stress or not, our blood pressure increases. However, when the conversation is stressful—*and especially when we hold our words inside*—our blood pressure can go to extremely high levels. This can be a dangerous situation, especially for people with a history of heart problems such as hypertension.

When a man learns to bridge both worlds—by speaking the language of the head and the language of the heart—it can make tremendously positive changes in his own life and the lives of those with whom he lives and works. Not only that, it can decrease the unnecessary stress that accompanies poor marital or business conversation. In the end, our hearts will thank us for the decreased workloads, and those around us will be thankful for the increased depth and feeling we have added to our communication.

But how does a woman actually help her husband bridge the "language" barrier in a home? If a man opens his eyes to several natural characteristics of his wife, he'll see that her natural strengths can complete him because. . . .

2. Women Tend to Relate on Multiple Levels

When most women are asked to describe the mental capacity of men, their response is, "He has a one-track mind." In a sense, that's pretty close—and not just in the area of sexual relationships. We men usually do concentrate on one thing at a time. It's as if our minds are like the inside of a battleship, with many different decks and compartments. When we leave one deck, we close the water-tight door to the last compartment and busy ourselves with what's close at hand.

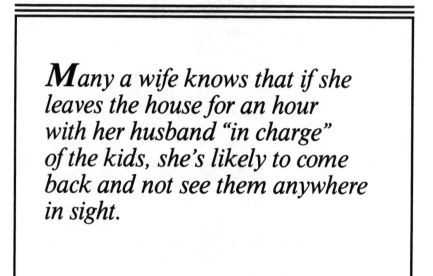

Many a wife knows that if she leaves the house for an hour with her husband "in charge" of the kids, she's likely to come back and not see them anywhere in sight.

That's one reason why a wife, when she asks her husband if he thought about her at work that day, is likely to hear:

"Did I think about you today? Well . . . I mean . . . I'm sure I *must* have thought about you sometime!" Take heart, ladies; it's probably not that he doesn't love you, it's just a reflection of his tendency to "compartmentalize" his thinking. A man tends to remain in one world at work that centers around the office or job-site, and when he leaves that one, he enters another that revolves around the family.

A woman's mind, though, is like the war room on that battleship. It's the nerve center, equipped with fancy electronic devices that allow it to monitor all the vital signs on every deck of the house at the same time. Because of the way her mind has been designed, its radar is constantly on and sweeping in all directions.

What this means is that the average woman misses very little about her environment, no matter how crowded it is. That same "radar" system that is so sensitive in Norma is what alerted our fishing guide's wife to the coming windstorm. And it's also the same system that makes it very difficult for the average woman to relax completely if her husband is watching the kids.

Many a wife knows that if she leaves the house for an hour with her husband "in charge" of the kids, she's likely to come back and not see them anywhere in sight. Then when she asks her husband (who's now in front of the television set) where they are, he's liable to say, "Oh, I don't know . . . they're around here somewhere. . . . I think they went down to the pond to play," as he turns back to his game.

She, on the other hand, usually knows exactly what's going on with the kids, no matter what time of day it is, or what part of the house they are in. It doesn't matter if she lives in a three-story Victorian mansion. She can be in the basement when her radar goes off, but she knows the kids are in the attic fighting.

Greg and Mike literally thought that Mom had the house wired when they were out. Invariably, they'd be as quiet as church mice doing something they shouldn't, and still Norma's radar would go off, and she'd catch them.

A woman misses very little about her environment, which is probably the basis for that mysterious gift some have called intuition. We feel strongly that it's more than a natural "hunch." It's just one more way in which a woman can complete her husband— and another reason a man should honor and value his wife.

3. Women Have the Unique Skill of Personalizing Their Environment

Another tremendous strength a woman has is to become personally involved with everything around her. For example, have you ever wondered why the average wife doesn't care that much about watching a football game with you? Most of the time, it's because she doesn't *know* any of the players. There's nothing "personal" going on down on the field. (Now, this may not be true when she is in the stands sitting with you and some friends, but for many women, the battling going on down on the field is not as interesting as who you meet coming and going to the game.)

One way to get a woman to be more interested in a sporting event is to "personalize" it. Take a few moments and share some information with her about one of the players ("Honey, see that guy who just caught the ball? He's the guy I told you about who's been really struggling with his wife and kids . . . "). Then she'll feel more a part of the game and what's going on because she has an emotional tie to it.

How strong is a woman's need for an "emotional" attachment to someone? One indication is the fact that in this country alone, over ten million romance novels will be purchased this year, and 97 percent of them will be bought by women. Why? At least in part because these stories offer a picture of intimacy and deep personal relationships that, unfortunately, many find too infrequently in their own lives.

If a man isn't aware of his wife's tendency to "personalize" almost everything around her, it can lead to friction in a home. That's because for most women, the cat is not just an "animal," but their first baby. The wallpaper isn't just "something to cover the walls," but a reflection of who she is.

As you may have noticed, many men tend to take certain things in their surroundings for granted. For example, the car they drive. Recently, a story appeared in *Reader's Digest* that I really enjoyed.

There was a man with several daughters who owned an old, decapitated convertible. For years, every woman in the house urged him to get rid of the "pile of junk" and even refused to ride in it with him in public. Then one day it happened. He walked out from work, and the car had been stolen.

The man's wife and daughters were celebrating that night that his eyesore of a car had been stolen when the phone rang. The party was over—the police had found the car.

"We found your car only about ten blocks from where they took it," the policeman said. "We don't know who did it, but they left a note saying, '*You can have it back. We'd rather walk!*'"

For a man, a car can often be in the worst of shape because, "It's just transportation" to him, but for a woman, if her car isn't washed it can often leave her feeling incomplete. Why is that? In part, it's because it's usually easier for a man to separate himself from his surroundings than it is for a woman.

This is especially true of the house or apartment you live in. To a man, the home is a place of rest. To a woman, it's an extension of herself.

That's why a woman may feel "trashy" if the trash hasn't been taken out; she may feel dirty if the floors aren't cleaned and the carpet not vacuumed; she may even feel broken down if the fence isn't fixed or the door is falling off the hinges. Each of these things is a part of her; when they aren't right, she feels as if something's not right with her.

Why is this something that can benefit or "complete" a man? In part, it's because a woman's natural sensitivity to her surroundings makes her alert to the things that surround us—and especially the people in her world.

It's like having a quality control expert in the home who can spot lurking problems with her "early warning" system. In addition, her heightened awareness of those around her rarely causes her to make a crucial relationship mistake many men make at the office—and at home.

4. Women Are Generally More Concerned about People Than They Are about Projects.

For the most part, men are conquerors. That means at least some of the time they tend to be less concerned about people and feelings than they are about "getting the job done." This is quite natural for men, because we tend to derive our sense of worth from what we do. The better "job" we do, the better we feel about ourselves.

Women, on the other hand, primarily derive their feelings of worth from those to whom they're related. If a woman is married, she looks to her husband more than any other earthly individual for her personal sense of value and worth.

That natural concern for deep and loving relationships that a woman has can certainly be shared by a man—but it can also be more easily set aside by him as well. Take hunting for example.

The average man can load up his high-powered rifle, go hunting, and blow away one of God's beautiful creatures. Then he can cut off its head, stuff it, hang it on a wall, gather his neighbors around, and triumphantly say, "I did that!" He's conquered something!

But generally women have already made much too deep an emotional attachment to Thumper and Bambi in the movie theater to execute one of their real-life counterparts out in the wild. When those sweet little animals die, a part of the woman is hurt as well.

You can even see this difference between the sexes when men and women go shopping. When the average man hears the average woman say, "Honey, let's go shopping and find a new blouse for me," he hears the word "shopping." But what she usually means is

"Shoooopppppppiiiiinnnng!"

Once a man hears her words, "Let's get a blouse," he is like a bloodhound who has just had an escaped prisoner's scent held in front of his nose. Once he's gotten a "whiff" of what he's going to the mall to hunt for, then it's off to sniff out a new blouse (any blouse), bag it, get back home, and lay on the porch as quickly as possible.

Since men are often more "conquer"-oriented than women, they usually tend to concentrate on the completion of a project—regardless of the personal costs. But because a woman's sense of value is so closely tied to all the relationships around her, she's often gifted in helping a man be more sensitive to what's really important beyond the immediate goal.

Take Brian, for example. For several Saturday mornings, his goal was to get up as early as he could, mow the yard, do his chores, shower, and get in front of the television set just before kickoff of the first football game of the day. As he attacked his objective of getting the yard done and getting in front of the television, he wasn't always concentrating on how to build a strong relationship with his six-year-old son, Mark.

Mark would get up with his father each Saturday and desperately try to help him with the yard. But try as he might, he could never keep up with his father on any of the chores. That was especially true when it came to "helping" his father dump all the grass from the catch bag into the trash can.

"Son, that's enough," Brian would finally say in frustration after having to pick up yet another pile of spilled yard clippings. "I don't need that kind of help right now. Why don't you go inside and see if you can help your mother? *Now.*"

Brian's wife watched each week as little Mark would walk out the door to help his Dad with his chest sticking out—and walk back in a short time later crest-fallen. As a loving wife, she brought what was happening to his attention.

At an appropriate time, she used a word picture[4] to explain to him the way he was killing his son's spirit in his "quest" to quickly mow the yard. He was sacrificing his relationship with his son for a football game that could easily be video-taped and played when his son was in bed. Fortunately, Brian was wise enough to accept her correction. He even expressed appreciation to his wife for what she said:

"Thanks, Honey. Now that you mention it, I've got to admit that I have been pushing Mark aside these past few weeks. I'm not sure why I get so caught up in getting something done my way, but I'm going to learn. My son is a lot more important to me than how quickly I get the chores done—no matter what game is on."

In Brian's home, a sensitive woman received extra honor that night because of her willingness to point out his steamroller tendencies to put projects in front of people. But that's not the only reason he's thankful for the woman God has given him. There's one more reason that outshines them all. Namely, in every marriage, right under a man's roof, is one of the most priceless things God has given him—one that he can tap into almost any time to help him in his responsibility to develop a close-knit family.

The Incredible Worth of a Woman: She Has a Built-In Marriage Manual

Do you know the main reason why men are held back from a promotion at work? Is it a lack of technical skill? Rarely. A lack of education? Occasionally. But the primary reason men fail to be promoted is their lack of relationship skills.[5]

What most men don't realize is that they have the world's greatest instructors in relationships living right under their roofs. A wife is a gold mine of relational skills. If a man wants to take advantage of the "missing part" of the nature that has affected every "Adam" since the beginning, all he has to do is look into the eyes of his wife—and learn to *tap into her built-in marriage manual.*

In talking personally with women in over sixty cities (where we've done our conferences these past five years), I've always asked for—but never found—a woman who was an exception to this rule. Namely, I have never met a woman who by her God-given nature didn't possess a built-in relationship manual.

So here's how a husband can tap into this rich source of relational skills to improve his own marriage—and his skills with his children and others as a result. First, a man needs to realize that his wife comes equipped with two tremendous inner strengths:

1. She has a strong, innate desire for a good and healthy relationship; and

2. She has the natural ability to recognize a great relationship.

These two underlying qualities are the basis for three important questions that a man can use to pull out of a woman her built-in relationship manual.

Three Questions That Can Help a Man Tap into a Woman's Built-In Marriage Manual

Three simple but life-changing questions are all it takes. For the sake of argument, let's say Bob is going to ask Julie these questions:

Julie, I realize that one way God equipped you as a helper was to complete me in the relational side of life. So let's begin with our marriage . . .

Question #1: On a scale from one to ten, with zero being terrible and ten being a great marriage, where would you like our relationship to be?

Naturally, almost every woman (and man, too!) answers that they'd like to consistently be around a nine or a ten. After all, how many of us are into misery? Bob would then go on to question two:

Question #2: On a scale from one to ten, overall, where would you rate our marriage today?

In most cases, a man will rate the marriage two to three points *higher* than his wife will, so don't let the initial difference in perception shock you. Remember, the average woman is much more in tune with the state of the relationship than the average man.

Be sure and give her time to think and share. Use the "quick listen" method described in Chapter 9 to reassure her that you value her opinion and want to understand her as much as possible.

Whether you agree with your wife or not, it's important to honor her by giving her your full attention. The goal is to understand her and to be open to what she may say.

The next question is the crucial one. In fact, in some ways it doesn't matter what she answers to Question Two, for the most important question is this third one—the one that can flip open the pages to her natural marriage and relationship manual.

Question #3: As you look at our relationship, what are some specific things we could do over the next six weeks that would move us closer to a ten?

I have yet to find a woman who cannot paint the answer to that question in brilliant detail. However, I have met numerous men who can't even find the paintbrush!

In some cases, your wife may be reluctant to answer this question, fearing she'll hurt your feelings—or even worse, that you'll hurt *her* feelings by your defensive response. That's why it's important to patiently give her the time to talk and to consistently reassure her about the security of your relationship—no matter what she says or where she rates things. If she feels secure in your love, almost without exception she'll be able to open up with many helpful specifics on how you can more effectively steward the gift of the marriage and family God has given you.

For any of us who are serious about effectively loving those who mean the most to us, honor must characterize our relationships. Nowhere is that more true than for the man who is serious about being a Christlike lover to his wife.

Let me state something clearly. *Valuing his wife's differences, and even tapping into her built-in marriage manual, does not transfer leadership or responsibility away from the husband and place it onto the wife.* Biblically, there is no escape clause from the man being the head of the home—the man is the fact-finder when it comes to building a strong relationship. But to be the type of loving leader God intended, allowing a wife to fulfill her God-given function as a loving "completer," is a must. It can help a man replace insensitivity with sensitivity, and lording it over others with genuine love for them. It can also help men become the observant servant leaders they were always meant to be.

By appreciating the unique and wonderful way God has created a woman, we can add a richness and joy to our marriage that virtually everyone wants, but very few have. The secret is in learning to honor a woman as someone unmatched in God's creation, made especially by Him as a completer, to do things for a man he could never do for himself.

Yet what do you do when your "completer" becomes discouraged or loses energy in your relationship? Or what happens when you do? In the next chapter, we'll see a second loving action that can be a tremendous help to a home. It involves learning a practical method of energizing your mate in as little as sixty seconds.

5

Energizing Your Mate in Sixty Seconds

My wife Norma has always loved zoos. Regardless of what type of zoo, or how many times she's been through it, she always thrills at the opportunity to go again. On the other hand, having been through dozens of zoos over the years, I rarely get excited about going through another one. But one day on a speaking trip to the Midwest, Norma picked up a brochure advertising a "Wild Animal Park" that actually attracted my attention.

When she saw I wasn't immediately saying "no," her face lit up. Her voice was full of excitement as she read me the brochure and said, "Gary, I know you'll like this one. Will you come with me? *Please.*" Once again, we were off to one of Norma's favorite places in life.

Before we could actually go, there was one minor problem we had to overcome. The brochure described this park as a "drive-through zoo" and we didn't have a car. So with a phone call, I arranged with my close friend and now ministry associate, Terry Brown, to borrow his car for the afternoon. He graciously agreed and delivered to us his tiny Fiat convertible within the hour, and we were on our way to the park.

As we drove up to the main gate, they said convertibles were allowed, but that we would have to keep the top up. The friendly park ranger also gave us some advice on how to feed the animals, when not to feed them, and a strong warning about the one place in the park where we had to keep the windows rolled up. This area was called a "danger zone" because of the very large or very wild animals living there. Emphatically, we were told:

"If anything happens to your car in this section of the park, just pull off the road and honk your horn and a friendly ranger will come and rescue you."

It sounded safe enough to me, so we began our self-guided

tour of the drive-through zoo. Once inside, we quickly discovered that the animals living there were particularly friendly. The giant birds tried to stick their heads inside the car looking for food. One giraffe did manage to stick his twenty-inch gray tongue inside the car and tried to slurp Norma's sandwich out of her lap. At this point I readily agreed with her that this was far better than a "regular" zoo.

Then it happened. Halfway through the park, we finally came to the well-marked "danger zone," and right when we were in the middle of no-man's land, Norma asked, "What's that coming out from under the hood?" Well, it was steam from our overheating radiator, and it was beginning to form an unwelcome white cloud!

"Oh no," I groaned. Glancing at the temperature gauge for the first time, I noticed that it was way beyond the "hot" reading on the gauge and nearing the "melt down" zone.

Great, I thought. *We've only been gone an hour and already I've ruined my friend's car.*

I started to pull over, but Norma cried out,

"You can't pull over here! Didn't you see that sign? *This is a danger zone!*"

"But honey, I can't wreck this man's car. I've *got* to pull over!"

"But not here!" she pleaded. "What if we're both trampled to death or eaten alive? Who'll take care of the children? . . ."

"Now, don't worry," I said as gently as I could. "It says right here in the brochure that if we have any trouble in a danger zone, all we have to do is honk the horn and a friendly ranger will come right over and rescue us!"

Norma frowned, but with the way the car was acting, it was obvious we didn't have any choice. So we pulled over, and I started honking the horn. . . . and honking. . . . and honking. . . .

I honked for forty-five minutes, and no friendly ranger ever came and rescued us. Basically, the guide at the gate had lied to us. We could have been eaten, trampled, or both. But what happened between Norma and me during this time illustrates one of the most important principles I've ever discovered when it comes to developing loving, lasting relationships.

"Don't Look Now, but. . . ."

While all my honking didn't alert a single ranger, it did notify every furry resident of the "danger zone" that we were there—and that we might have (or become) lunch. First, the wild burros ambled up and began nibbling at the top of my friend's convertible. I finally had to get out of the car and yell and chase them away to convince them that hay would be better than our fabric top. I had just gotten back inside the car when I made the mistake of looking into the rear view mirror.

"Norma," I said in my calmest voice, "don't look now, but you're never going to believe what's coming!"

An entire herd of huge, shaggy buffalo were walking out of the woods and soon surrounded our little Fiat. One of them, on my side of the car, wandered over, knelt down, and put his head right up against my window. With those great big brown eyes and a huge head about four inches from my face (the steam coming out of his nose began fogging my window), it was obvious he was saying nonverbally, "Got anything in there for me?"

Then he started pushing on the window, rocking the car as he did. During the whole ordeal, neither of us looked up, hoping our ignoring them would make them go away.

"Listen to that thing breathe!" I said.

"That's not him breathing," Norma said. *"That's me!"*

Finally, our hairy friends wandered off, and our car cooled down enough for us to drive to the main gate for help.

As funny as it seems now, that hour trapped in the car together was actually a very tense situation. In fact, if it had been several years earlier, one or both of us might have responded in a very different way. We could have easily used that tense situation to explode and so weaken our relationship, rather than relying on an important principle that could strengthen it.

Norma could have said to me, "Gary, I can't handle this! I don't care if this thing explodes, get this car moving!" or I could have easily said to her, "Be quiet! You're going to see a wild animal inside this car if you don't hush up!"

Either of us could have done and said things to each other in the "heat of battle" that we would have later regretted; and if we had blown up, it would have drained away the positive feelings and energy we'd stored up in our marriage for weeks as quickly as the water draining from our radiator.

On this trip, however, things were different. They were different because we had finally begun to understand and practice an incredibly important concept in the Scriptures.

We never know when we're going to find ourselves in a frustrating situation with someone we love. During these times, when a high-intensity predicament is threatening to drain the positive energy right out of our relationships, most of us take one of two roads. We either choose to react and blast those near us or we choose to respond in a way that actually helps to strengthen our marriage. It all begins with learning how to energize your mate during a stressful situation in as little as sixty seconds.

Energizing Your Mate in Sixty Seconds

What is the biblical principle that kept our emotions in check during this difficult time? It's really an incredible power that is right at our fingertips—the ability to be gentle and to tenderly touch each other.

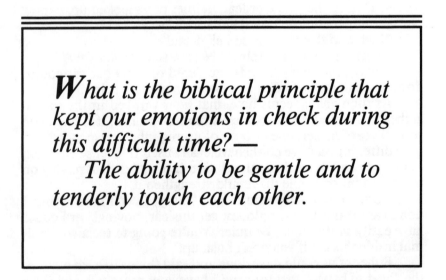

What is the biblical principle that kept our emotions in check during this difficult time?—
The ability to be gentle and to tenderly touch each other.

For years I had known intellectually that "a soft answer turns away anger" (Proverbs 15:1), and that a key fruit of the spirit was "gentleness" (Galatians 5:23). But I had never applied either principle in my most important relationships. Now, if softness as a way to energize a person sounds too easy to you, how often do you feel gentle in the middle of catastrophe?

Most people's basic bent during times of stress is to lash out or lecture—or both— especially if the predicament is somebody else's fault. But tenderness, above and beyond the call of our human nature, is a transformer, an energizer of those around us.

Since I wasn't fortunate enough to have a father who knew how to be tender to his wife, I wasn't aware that softness during stressful times was even an option until several years into my marriage. And that's when I learned that one of a person's greatest needs is to be comforted, especially during those moments in life when the roof falls in.

A Creative Way to Add a Skylight to Your Home. . . .

One afternoon I was very late coming home from boating with my son Greg. I had taken the car, which left Norma with only our mini-motor home for transportation. She waited and waited, but when I was several hours later than I had predicted, she decided to take our mini-motor home to the grocery store.

Granted, our motor home is not the easiest thing to handle in the world. I'd already had my share of close calls when it came time to park or back the vehicle out. But Norma re-defined the word "close-call" as she tried to back the camper out of the driveway.

She had almost made it out from under the carport when she turned the wheel the wrong way and sheared off an entire section of the roof. And if that wasn't bad enough, the falling roof bounced off the hood of the camper, scraping away paint and leaving a deep dent in its wake.

When I pulled into the driveway an hour later, I couldn't believe my eyes. Looking at the gaping hole in the roof, my first response was to look at the sky to see if the tornado was still around, but one look at our mobile home told me that it was Mother Norma, not Mother Nature, who had caused this catastrophe.

I instantly felt like ordering her out of the house and asking her questions like, "Where did you get your driver's license? From a gumball machine at Shop-Mart?!"

Instead, I sat in my car, frozen, with my hands on the steering wheel, praying, "Lord, you have to give me strength.

Every fiber in my body wants to lecture my wife now and not be gentle with her. This is one of those pressure situations, and I know I have a choice. Lord, help me figure out what I'm going to do." Turning to my son Greg I asked him, "What do you think I ought to do?"

Greg said, "Dad, why don't you do what you teach?"

"That's a good idea," I said.

But all the while I was praying for the strength to be tender. Being tender at such a moment is definitely not natural. You have to take off the comfortable old nature of lectures and anger, and put on the new nature of tenderness. This can be excruciatingly difficult (Ephesians 4:22–24).

Finally, I got out of the car and walked toward the piece of roof lying in the driveway, but just as I got up to the camper, Norma came flying around the side of the house.

I fought off the voice ringing in my mind, *Lecture her! Lecture her!* and I did what didn't feel "natural" at the time. I simply held her in my arms and gently patted her on the back. I hadn't spoken one word when finally, Norma pulled away and said, "Oh, look what I did! I wrecked the motor home and knocked off the roof," she said. Then she added, "And I told the neighbors across the street what I did, and they're watching to see how you're going to respond."

Thankfully, I hadn't given the neighbors anything to gossip about by exploding at Norma. I just put my arms around her again and gently called her by my favorite affectionate name for her:

"Norm, listen. You know I love you. You're more important to me than campers and roofs. I know you didn't do this on purpose, and you're feeling really bad about it."

At that very moment, I could feel Norma relaxing. What's more, I immediately felt better myself as my own anger drained out of me to be replaced by feelings of tenderness. While it's hard to explain, I could tell that instead of being pulled apart, we were actually growing *stronger* as a result of the trial.

After a few more minutes of talking and holding her, Norma went on with whatever she was doing, and I went out to the garage to lay my hands on the few tools I had. After taking a deep breath, I said to Greg, "Well, I'd better get at it."

Just then, from out of nowhere, a friend from my church pulled up into our driveway. This wasn't just any ordinary friend. He was a local contractor pulling up in his pickup filled with hammers, saws, lumber, nails, paint, and a long ladder. He jumped out and said, "OK, Gary. Let's get at it!"

"Where did you come from?" I asked in disbelief.

Apparently our good neighbors across the street weren't only watching my reactions to Norma. They had also been calling everyone around town to talk about our hole in the roof. Ironically, my friend had been one of the first to hear the news. With his expert help, and without exaggeration, we had our impromptu skylight patched and re-painted within two hours.

As I went to bed that night with Norma snuggled up next to me, I was amazed that I had actually done something right for a change, during a stressful situation. What would I have normally done? I could have zapped the life right out of her emotionally with angry words and lectures, and it would have taken days for us to feel our way back to each other.

If I hadn't known about the power of gentleness, I'm sure I would have acted as I had in the past and blown up. This time I didn't, and amazingly, it made all the difference. The old Gary Smalley might have lost it. The new one followed a biblical blueprint for turning away anger, and it made even a stressful event a time of closeness.

I learned an important lesson that day; it's one I've seen repeated time and time again in my life and in the lives of others. Simply put, that lesson is:

Remaining tender during a trial is one of the most powerful ways to build an intimate relationship (James 1:19, 20).

The power of tenderness is outlined and illustrated from one end of the New Testament to the other. However, from my perspective, Ephesians 4 does the best job of explaining it. In this section of Scripture:

• Verse 15 introduces the concept of gentleness by challenging us to grow up in all aspects "into Jesus Christ." We're to grow up in love and to become mature. That's what each of us wants I'm sure—to be mature, caring people who can encourage those around us.

• Then verses 22 and 23 tell us that to become complete in Christ, we're to take off our "old self," which is the opposite of godliness, and then put on our "new self." Now the question is, what is it we take off and what do we put on in its place?

• While there are certainly many aspects of our fallen nature that need to be exchanged for godly characteristics, verse 29 gives us one specific we can begin to put into practice today. Without pulling any punches, it says we are not to let "any unwholesome word proceed out of our mouth." Unwholesome words popping out of our mouths are a reflection of our old nature, and they need to be replaced with their opposite—words that are tender, gentle, and nurturing.

The verse continues with the encouragement to speak only words that are "good for edification according to the need of the moment, that it may give grace to those who hear." These are words that build up or strengthen others, words that bring energy and life to people.

Let's look at several practical ways to energize your mate, children, and friends on a daily basis by learning to replace angry, deflating lectures with tender, strengthening words.

Lectures and Tenderness Don't Mix

Let's say a woman is losing emotional energy and reaches the end of her rope. In frustration, she might say to her husband:

"Oooh, I've had it around this house. *Look at this mess.* Nobody ever picks up anything around here. I've got to have some help!"

Now that's a clear sign of a woman who is losing energy. The problem is, her husband may hear only the words, "I need help," and not the feelings or issues behind her frustration. Once a man hears the words, "I need help," his natural desire is to solve the problem at hand. Instantly, he's capable of taking over and saying something like this:

"Honey, I'm really glad you brought this up. You know, if you could just get organized around here, you wouldn't be so frustrated. It's about time you got a system of housework like we have at the office. And by the way, are you still taking those vitamin pills we spent all that money for? Are you getting your rest on a regular basis?"

Or worse yet, we men are capable of hitting below the belt and saying something like, "*Honey, do you think you're being disorganized is an indication that you're not spending enough time in God's Word on a regular basis?"*

Lectures are so natural. Particularly when they make us conquering males feel like we're solving a problem. The real problem, though, is that we've missed the deeper message *behind* her words. In fact, if we do give her a management-effectiveness course on cleaning the house, she tends to resent us, not applaud us. That often leads to a man saying something like:

"Well, what's wrong with you? If you don't want my help, then why did you ask me!"

The problem is, *she never was asking for help in the first place!* At least not the type of help that comes from lectures and object lessons. It only sounded that way because he focused on the words alone. Like many women, this wife was sharing her underlying feelings, her hurt, and her need for support, but what she expressed was her frustration. What a woman needs during times of expressed frustration is not a husband's mouth, but his shoulder. She really needs to be comforted and encouraged. She needs energizing—with a nice dose of meaningful touching tossed in.

We need to understand that when someone is going through a trial, they sometimes express that emotional draining of energy through their anger, discouragement, hurt feelings, or anxiety. The last thing a friend, spouse, or child who's hurting wants from us is a lecture, especially one that's delivered in harshness and anger.

Not only females resist or react to lectures or harsh words. Let's say it's been a very frustrating day at the office and a typical man walks in complaining, "This job doesn't pay enough for what they make me go through." In most cases, he's sharing his frustration—not issuing an invitation to be criticized. Not many men would enjoy hearing their wives say, "Yeah, they *don't* pay you enough, all right. You need to get a real job that pays more so we can make ends meet. In fact, I'll tell you what kind of job you *ought* to get. . . ."

The same thing is true with children. Teenagers rarely appreciate coming home after flunking a test and being met with angry, challenging words. I'm not saying that you can't confront a person in love over areas of error in his or her life, but at the *moment of vulnerability,* and particularly in the midst of the crisis itself, what a person needs first is tenderness.

Tenderness acts as a firebreak to an advancing forest fire. Fire-fighters get ahead of the fire, then clear a wide trail free of all "flammable" material. The fire may roar up to the firebreak, but it can't jump across and keep burning. That's one tremendous benefit of tenderness.

It takes work to "strip" an area clear of emotional kindling —particularly when a fiery trial is closing in on us. But we can head off the negative emotions that are coming and keep from getting "burned" if we do. Or, as we mentioned, we can add more fuel to the already burning fire—in the form of lectures.

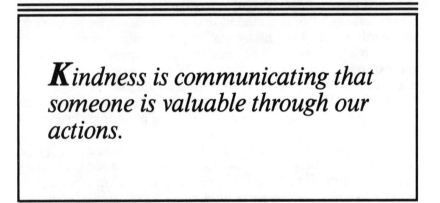

*K*indness is communicating that someone is valuable through our actions.

To use another word picture, lectures act as an electronic suction device that can suck out all our energy, leaving us emotionally, spiritually, and physically drained. I've sat in numerous counseling sessions where a man was criticizing his wife or vice versa, and you can almost hear the suction machine roaring, pulling the life right out of their relationship.

Lectures may seem right, and occasionally they are an appropriate response to a person, but tender, honoring, "edifying" words can head off an argument before it breaks out in our relationship.

Making Tenderness a Habit in Your Home

Okay, I hear what you're saying: "I'd like to be more tender-hearted. But it's still a little abstract. How about several concrete suggestions on how to practice this new gentle habit?"

Ephesians 4:32 is your instruction booklet for becoming a tenderhearted person. In these verses are two powerful ways to be tenderhearted. The first is, "Be kind . . . to one another," then, "forgiving each other, just as God in Christ forgave you."

In other words, when it comes to being tender, kindness, gentleness, and forgiveness are like battery packs. They are what gives tenderness its punch. Let's look at each of these steps more closely.

Have you ever wondered what being "kind" to someone really means? *Kindness is communicating that someone is valuable through our actions.* There are ways to be kind—like visiting friends at the hospital or going to their home after the loss of a loved one. In these cases, kindness is usually best spoken without a word—by a hug, or a gentle act or touch. Our presence alone says, "I'm so sorry; you're very special to me; I'm praying for you." Combine a "kind" act with a tender touch, and the results can be life-changing.

Recently John Trent and I were on a radio program in California talking about the importance of being "tenderhearted," when a man called in and told us an incredible story about the power of silent tenderness.

A few years back, the caller had had a major heart attack. Though he was only in his early fifties at the time, it was so serious, the doctors at the hospital told his wife to notify the family he probably wouldn't live for more than a few days.

When his seventy-year-old father was called, he flew cross-country to be at what he thought was his son's deathbed. The fact that his father had come at all was a tremendous encouragement to his son. In all his life, he had never once heard the words, "I love you," from his father. Deep down, he always felt he was loved, but for years, he had longed to actually hear the words that would prove he was valuable to his father.

"My father never did come right out and say he loved me," he said. "But after he came out to see me in the hospital, I knew he did—and all because of one thing he did when I was lying in that hospital bed."

"What was it he did?" we asked, glued to our headphones.

"When I was in the hospital," the man continued, "my dad walked in and without saying a word, he took my hand and gently held it for over half an hour. He was tender with me for the first time I can ever remember. He still couldn't bring himself to *say,* 'I love you,' but I know now he really did."

We all teared up just listening to the emotion in his voice as he told us his story. As powerful a story as this was, it was "the rest of the story" that hit us the hardest, for the man went on to tell us that he miraculously recovered from his heart attack. But three days after he had come to visit his son in the hospital, the seventy-year-old *father* passed away!

This man shared with us and the entire listening audience, "If my father had never shown me his love by that one tender act, I don't think I would ever have truly known how much he loved me, but that one act of gentleness spoke more to me than anything he could have said. . . ."

His father's actions communicated kindness in its purest form. Without words—simply by his gentle touch—he shouted out the concept of tenderness in words that will forever ring in his son's heart.

Tenderness and Timing

Often the time to give someone a gentle word of encouragement or a meaningful touch is obvious. Sometimes, though, especially for people like me who do not come from a "high touch" background, it's hard to recognize the not-so-obvious times we need to be tender. What do we do then?

I'll never forget what one woman told me:

"If my husband would only put his arms around me and hold me when I'm feeling blue, and not give me a nonstop lecture or pep-talk about 'counting it all joy,' it would transform our marriage."

"Have you ever *told* him what you need?" I asked.

"Are you kidding? He'd be embarrassed and so would I," she laughed.

"This may come as a surprise to you," I said, "but he probably doesn't know how to be tender with you. He's been trained to lecture. Perhaps he needs some training in what genuine tenderness is."

"That makes sense to me," she said. "Many times when I'm crying and upset, he'll ask, 'What do you want me to *do?*' And I just flare up and say, '*If I have to tell you what to do, then that would ruin it!*'"

A husband should ask his wife, and a wife her husband, to define "tenderness" in their own terms. How he should hold her for her to feel safe and loved—when is the best time for her to be soft and sympathetic with him? A wife or husband shouldn't expect his or her mate to be a mind-reader when it comes to meeting the very important needs in this area.

Most of us aren't good emotional mind-readers anyway, and too few of us come from comforting backgrounds so we don't know the nonverbal signals that say, "Please hold me." While attempting to talk about being tender may seem awkward at first, just being willing to talk about this much needed area tends to bring energy and life to a relationship.

Using Tenderness as an Important Protective Tool for Your Children

We've talked about the need both a woman and man have for tenderness—a willingness to decrease our lectures and increase our tender expressions of love, but if gentleness is a key to marital growth, it is equally powerful when practiced between parent and child.

I know a man who had a very strained relationship with his teenage daughter. Recently, she had been dating a boy he did not care for, and her father had been extremely cutting in expressing his feelings. In fact, every time he brought up the subject (and everything they talked about seemed somehow to lead into it), their exchanges became loud and dishonoring.

At our seminar, he realized for the first time how important tenderness was, and how little of it he was showing to his daughter. He decided that he had to begin putting on the new nature of encouraging words. He still disapproved of the boy his daughter was dating—but he didn't have to blast his daughter at close range every night with angry words just to vent his frustration.

That very night at the seminar, he prayed to be more gentle with his daughter—and the opportunity to put his prayer into practice came to pass. After he got home from the seminar, he walked upstairs to get ready for bed. He passed by his daughter's room and heard her crying as she talked over the phone. It was the boyfriend he disliked so much calling, and it was obvious that they were breaking up over the phone.

Inside, this father felt like jumping for joy. He couldn't think of anything better than what was happening, but something stopped him as he began to enter his daughter's room and pull out the standard "I told you he was a jerk" lecture. As he heard his daughter crying as she hung up the phone, he remembered his vow to God to bring tenderness into his home.

He walked slowly into her room and gently sat down on her bed. She lay with her head buried in her pillow. When she realized he was sitting next to her, she instantly bristled—figuring she knew what was coming, but her father said nothing. Instead, he quietly held her as she cried. When she finally stopped, she looked up at him and said, "Daddy, thank you for just being here with me."

As my friend walked out of his daughter's room, his emotions hit like a sheet of ice water. He realized that he had been so distant from his daughter for so long, it had been years since she had called him "Daddy."

The Master's Use of Tenderness

Our children, our spouse, our close friends, and each of us have a physical and emotional need for tenderness, expressed as words or as meaningful touches. Kindness comes from *honoring* that need in the lives of our loved ones and demonstrating that *love* by doing all we can to fulfill it.

The main reason I've mentioned tenderness and kindness as the second act of love is its great importance in communicating value to others. One of the loudest cries we hear among men, women, and children is the desperate plea for tenderness and gentleness from people who love them.

Jesus was the master at using tenderness to express high value to others. Remember how He greeted the children who came to Him? Mobbed by onlookers and protected by His disciples, Jesus could have easily waved to them from a distance or just ignored them altogether. He did neither. Jesus touched and blessed the children (Matthew 19:13).

His tenderness in dealing with others was graphically displayed when a leper came to Him, described in Luke as a man "with leprosy. . . . Jesus reached out his hand and touched the man" (Matthew 8:3).

To touch a leper in Jesus' day was to flirt with contracting the most terrifying terminal illness known to the biblical world. To have leprosy was to die shunned and untouched, driven away from civilization until finally, mercifully, you died. People in

Jesus' day would literally not get within a stone's throw of a leper—and Jewish law allowed stones to be thrown at a leper if he or she did come any closer.[1]

Yet even before Jesus spoke to the leper, He reached out His hand and touched him. Can't you imagine the people around Jesus recoiling from the sight? *No one* would touch a leper. Yet Jesus, in His wisdom, knew the man's heart, and his need for both spiritual cleansing and physical tenderness (see Matthew 8:1–3 and Luke 5:12).

When Tenderness Is Tied to Forgiveness

I've mentioned several aspects of being "tenderhearted." The first is kindness, and the second is meaningful touch. There is a third element of tenderness, though, that can have incredible power in relationships, namely *forgiving* one another.

It was years before I discovered what "forgiveness" means in the original language, but its meaning has always stayed with me. The literal picture behind the word "forgiveness" is untying a knot.[2] In the confines of everyday life, we can all get tied up in knots because of what others (especially our spouses) have said or done to us.

Part of forgiving someone is actually helping them become untied from their frustrations. No matter if the offense was big or small, forgiveness is saying, "I want this person free! Released! Untied!" For those who want to give encouragement and energy to their spouse or someone else, it can have incredible results.

A doctor friend of mine told me a story about a man who was dying in a nearby hospital. He was very, very ill, and the doctors could give him only hours to live. To all around him he seemed to have given up the fight, but that afternoon, this man's brother appeared in his room. The brother was the same one with whom he had never gotten along and who had always been rough and unkind to him growing up.

"I . . . I just come to ask if you will forgive me for the way I have treated you," the man's brother blurted out. Then he did an extraordinary thing. The rough brother took his dying brother's hand and told him he loved him.

At first when the brother sat and held the sick man's hand, it was rigid and stiff from the years of resentment he'd harbored against his brother. But remarkably, in the moments that followed those extraordinary words, his hand relaxed and the strength of his grip increased.

A moment before, he had felt so weak he did not think he could make it through the night. Yet after that visit, the sick brother steadily recuperated. The doctor couldn't pin-point any single thing that led to his rapid recovery. He told me that there could have been a number of physiological reasons for the man's strange and quick recovery. However, he felt sure that his brother's appearance and this man's recovery were not accidental. Namely, his brother's touch—and especially his words of forgiveness—were an important part in giving this man the energy to have a fighting chance to live.[3]

Are you still hesitating at knocking down old walls of anger and putting in a doorway of tenderness to your home—a door that opens to energizing words, gentle touching, and courageous forgiving? Then start this way.

Begin by spending time listening to your spouse, your child, or your friend—without any lectures. Then, the next time they show signs of losing energy in the midst of a discouraging or pressure-packed time, walk over and, without a word, put your arm around them or gently put your hand on their shoulder.

If you must say something, just say something like, "I can see you're really hurting, and I want you to know that I'm very sorry," or "I'm not sure if I can help you in what you're going through, but I love you, and if you're up to it, you can tell me how you're feeling." Particularly if tenderness hasn't been a hallmark of your relationships, you'll be amazed at how quickly being soft with people in this way can bring positive results.

I often tell people it doesn't take great wisdom to energize a person, but it does take sixty seconds. That's the amount of time it takes to walk over and gently hold someone we love. A few seconds invested in being tender can not only help our relationships —it can become catching in a home as well. But the amazing part of tenderness is that it works wonders even when we're not near our loved ones.

Once, while I was on a speaking trip, my schedule put me out of town on Mother's Day. I called Norma on that special day, telling her how sorry I was not to be there.

"How's your day been?" I asked.

"It's been a horrible day. Mike and Greg have been terrible to me, and everything's gone wrong." Resisting the temptation to tell her "exactly" what to do to make things "right," I simply listened. Soon, she slowed down, and I could tell she felt a bit better.

So I said, "Oh, I wish I was there with you." I said, "I'd just give you a great big hug, ummmmmmmm! In fact," I said, "put your arms around yourself and give yourself a big hug for me. Ummmmmmmmm!"

Now I didn't expect her to say, "Oh, you're such a wonderful husband. Thanks for being so tender." Wives usually don't say that when they're hurting. You've got to do this by faith because there may be times when they say, "Aw, you don't mean that!"

Just as I was getting off the phone, I heard the sound of a door opening, and Norma gasping in delight, "Ohhhh, Greg! They're so beautiful!"

"What's so beautiful?" I asked.

"Greggy brought me flowers for Mother's Day!"

"Hey, that's great," I said. Then it dawned on me.

"Say, Norma. Let me talk to Greg a minute."

Once my son was on the phone, I asked him where he got the flowers.

"Oh, I ordered them from a florist."

At that time he was only about thirteen years old, so I said, "But how did you pay for them?"

He said, "Oh, I just used your charge card, Dad."

Let's just say, I tried to remember all about showing tenderness to my son when I got home.

Tenderness is catching when it's communicated in a home —whether it's shared by an encouraging word, a gentle touch, or with an act of forgiveness. And the result between loved ones is energy—and another important way to build a loving, lasting relationship.

It takes practice and relying on God's strength to put on this important aspect of our new nature, but it's worth every ounce of effort we put into harnessing the power of tenderness to energize our loved ones.

As I mentioned earlier, energizing your mate by being gentle and tender is an important act of love, but it doesn't stand alone. It's just one of several ways we can put honor into action and show others how much we love them.

In the next chapter, I'm going to discuss an unbelievably powerful emotion that all of us have, yet few of us master. It's as much a part of our human makeup as our instinct for survival. It shapes the course of human events just as a roaring river carves canyons in sandstone. In addition, it has the potential to make our lives more meaningful and our relationships more fulfilling—or it can literally destroy the very things that are most precious to us.

Understanding it, like understanding the importance of tenderness, is absolutely essential if we want to honor God and others. Let's discover the secrets to mastering what may be the most powerful of all human emotions.

6

A Closed Spirit: Overcoming a Major Destroyer of Relationships

Late one night, while I was sound asleep, the phone rang. It was a man calling long distance who had gotten my number from a close friend. As I was struggling to wake up, he said, "Gary, I'm sorry to call so late, but my wife has left me. Actually, she's thrown me out of the house! She's so hostile toward me, it shocked me. I really didn't see it coming. We've been married almost twenty-five years, and now she's put me out on the street!"

As he continued, he asked, "Could you help me get back together with my wife?"

He sounded so desperate over the phone, I decided to help him if I could. So I asked, "Before I know if I can do anything to help you, I need to talk to your wife."

He immediately shot back, "That's impossible. She's not talking to me. She's not even talking to anyone who knows me. Gary, I don't think you understand. She *hates* me. You have no idea how much she hates me. She has a court order against me right now so that I can't even get into my own home!"

Having talked with many people in similar situations, I replied, "Well, I'll tell you what. I've never been turned down yet by a woman I've called. This could be the first time, but I'm willing to give it a try if you are."

After a brief pause, he said, "Well . . . I have nothing to lose, but please call me back the minute you talk to her and let me know what happens."

The next morning, I did call his wife. When she answered, I said, "Hello, I'm Gary Smalley. Your husband called me last night and really wanted some help, but I told him that in order to do anything for him, I would need to talk to someone who knows him as well as his wife. I was wondering. Could you just spend a couple of minutes with me, helping me understand your husband and why it was so difficult to live with him?"

Instantly she said, "Ohhhhh, I hate that man so much! I don't want to talk about him. In fact, even thinking about him upsets me."

I said, "It must have been horrible living with a man like that."

"You have no *idea* how horrible it was to live with that guy," she steamed. "He was so controlling, it was like I had to get *permission* to go to the bathroom!"

"How did you endure that kind of treatment for so many years?" I asked, trying everything I could just to keep her on the phone!

"I don't know how I managed, and now you're getting me to talk about him—and I don't want to talk about him!"

In the end, she did share several specific things this man had done—beginning with their honeymoon. Many were small, inconsiderate actions that had piled up hurt feelings until molehills became mountains.

After talking with her for only five minutes, I thanked her profusely for sharing her thoughts and time with me and hung up. Immediately I called her husband.

"Did you talk with her?" he asked.

"Yes," I said, "and you're right. *You are in big trouble!*"

Over the years, I could number in the hundreds the husbands who have called or written with a similar story. In each case, the man never "realized" that he was in such bad shape until his marital world came crashing down around him.

While there are unique situations with each person that has called, I can think of one common element in every case. In fact, it's one of the major destroyers of families—*unresolved anger.* Anger, though, is such a "normal" human emotion. How can it be so devastating to a relationship?

Opening the Door to a Major Destroyer of Families

Recently, a close friend told me about a rock star who brought home a cute little lion cub to raise on his ranch in Tennessee. Of course, he had to hire a lawyer to convince the local zoning board to give him a special permit to own a wild animal as a "pet," but with money being no object, he managed to get that detail taken care of quickly enough.

For several years his "tame" lion was quite a hit with his house guests. It never acted like a dangerous predator, only like a big, playful pet. Then one day without warning, a parent's worst nightmare became this man's reality.

His little two-year-old son was playing near the lion cage. The parents heard his screams for help from inside the house, but there was nothing they could do. The lion had broken out of his cage and brutally mauled the little boy before running off into the woods. In a terrible tragedy, the man's son died before they could even get him to the hospital.

I'm sure this man loved his son, and having raised the lion from a cub, he probably never consciously thought that it would one day rob his child of life. But all the reasoning in the world on why it was "safe" to keep a wild animal around the house couldn't erase that animal's nature. For centuries, people have learned the hard way about the dark side of a lion's nature. By allowing a predator into his home, the man was setting the stage for a potential tragedy.

I can't think of a single person I've met who would willingly expose a child or spouse to the fury of a full-grown lion, but I know of many husbands and wives who are letting another deadly killer walk right through their front door without a fight —*unhealthy, unresolved anger.*

Anger can rip the heart right out of a relationship. Without exaggeration, every hour that anger is allowed to stay in a person's life, it acts like an emotional time bomb ticking down to detonation. Like a terrorist bomb placed in an innocent looking shopping bag, it cares nothing for whom it hurts or eventually kills.

"But everyone gets angry. Even Jesus got 'angry' at the people in the temple," some may say. While this is certainly true, there is a major difference between righteous anger (that can have a "corrective" effect on error), and the kind of unhealthy anger that grows wild and, unchallenged, leads to destructive conflicts.

Like that rock star's lion, anger inside a person can never be made a "tame" emotion. Even "righteous anger" can become corrupted if a person is not very, very careful.

The man who called me in the middle of the night learned a crucial skill needed in any healthy relationship. In his case it proved to be a life-saving skill. He realized that by letting anger build up in his wife's life—anger that he was directly responsible for provoking—he had *closed her spirit* toward him.[1]

Like that innocent looking lion cub, he had let his insensitive acts pile up until they finally broke full force on the relationship. What he learned, however, actually helped him begin to repair the damage. He learned how to reopen his wife's closed spirit by getting the anger out of her life—and it made a dramatic change in his situation.

> *... we'll never be successful in our most important relationships until we learn how to drain the anger out of another person's life.*

Unfortunately, my late night friend is not unique. Parents can sometimes leave anger in a child's life when he or she is young, closing the child's spirit to them tightly. These same parents then see that deep-seated anger turns into resistance and rebelliousness in their teenagers. Employers can even close the spirit of their employees and soon meet resistance and a stiffening will in them.

Even though anger is potentially destructive, it can be dealt with, even in cases that may seem humanly impossible. That's what we're going to talk about in this chapter. We don't have to live in continual disharmony with others. We can literally be in harmony with those around us the majority of the time.

But we'll never be successful in our most important relationships until we learn to drain the anger out of another person's life. It's absolutely crucial that we learn how to "open" a person's closed spirit and get back in harmony with them again.

That begins as we learn the skills of putting unresolved anger out of our homes.

Putting Unresolved Anger out of a Home

First, let me define what I mean by unhealthy anger. *Selfish anger is the negative emotion we feel when a person or situation has failed to meet our needs, blocked our goals, or fallen short of our expectations.* It's what we feel when we've placed our needs, wants, and desires ahead of anyone else's. Then we become frustrated if those around us don't react the way we want them to. Let me illustrate more clearly what I mean by "negative" anger by giving a hypothetical example from my own home.

If I walk through the door one night and blast Norma for being five minutes late with dinner, I'd be absolutely wrong. It certainly isn't a sin for her to have dinner ready a few minutes late, and so to "let her have it" only demonstrates I was more interested in my own stomach than her welfare. That's the real problem with anger; it puts "me" ahead of everyone else and shows its displeasure whenever "I" don't get my way.

To clarify even further, there are two things we need to keep in balance. *First,* there is a "righteous" anger that stands up against sin. In Ephesians 4, there is a clear command to be angry over the things that would grieve God's heart (often the kinds of things that fill our newspapers and evening news). "*. . . But in your anger do not sin*" (Ephesians 4:26). Biblically, two wrongs never equal one right. Even if we become righteously angry over some anger-producing situation in our life or the lives of others, we are never justified in reacting in a sinful way.

Second, try as we might by logical reason, we will not always be able to avoid an immediate emotion. If someone accidentally steps on our foot or cuts in front of us on the freeway, our instantaneous reaction may be anger. There's nothing wrong or sinful about anger at this point. But when we let anger remain in our lives, or when we take its energy and direct it toward another person to hurt them, we move from a normal, healthy feeling to a destructive one.

Apply what Martin Luther used to say to negative thoughts: "You can't keep the birds from flying over your head . . . but you can keep them from building a nest in your hair!" We may not be able to keep anger from cropping up as an instantaneous and instinctive reaction to some pain or problem, but we can make a decision to keep it from staying in our lives and poisoning our attitudes or the attitudes of our loved ones.

Putting Healthy Limits on an Unhealthy Emotion

Let's go back to the couple with whom we started this chapter. From the time they were first married, this husband never placed any boundaries around his anger. Whenever his wife blocked any of his goals, or slowed him down in any way, he blasted her without regard to the emotional impact of his words.

One could say that his wife should have been more "spiritually mature" and should not have been hurt by his angry outbursts, but in real life, after a constant stream of angry words and actions over the years, she began to wilt under his treatment. This wife didn't realize that it is possible to be free from anger on our own, as you'll see in Chapters 13 and 14, and her husband didn't realize two things about anger in a home that can cripple a relationship.

1. Anger Eats Away at a Person's Health

Inside the brain, the decision you make to harbor negative feelings toward others can set off a series of physical events you would do well to avoid. When a person becomes angry, his body goes on "full alert." When the inner brain gets the message that there's a stressful situation out there, it doesn't ask questions—it reacts. Your body can easily release as many chemicals and disrupt as many bodily functions when you are angry with your spouse as if you're being attacked by a wild animal.[2]

After several years of living with an angry man, the woman in our story began manifesting several of the symptoms of a person with deep-seated anger locked inside them: early morning awakening, depression, tension, grinding teeth, an unexplainable sense of dread, jumpiness, and increased irritability.[3] None of these negative outworkings of anger is physically helpful. In fact, unresolved anger actually pulls a person's resistance to illness down.

When a person's body is constantly tense and on edge (for unrighteous anger never fully lets a person relax—even in his sleep), this tension will inevitably begin to wear the person down. That's when really undesirable things begin to happen physiologically, such as clinical depression, colitis, bleeding ulcers, anxiety attacks, lowered resistance to colds and flu, and heart and respiratory failure. Several researchers even believe that some types of cancer result from the mega-doses of stress that unhealthy anger carries with it.[4]

Perhaps all these physical manifestations of anger are behind the first commandment with a promise, "Honor your father and mother, so that you may live long . . . "(Exodus 20:12). Anger, however, doesn't just contribute to a poor grade on a health report card. It can also keep us "in the dark" when it comes to loving God and others.

2. The Greatest Problem of All

In 1 John 2:9–11, the apostle says that continual anger toward another results in losing the ability to live in God's light. Being angry with our brother pushes us into darkness—completely isolated from the light of His love. When we live with anger—or provoke it in the hearts of others—we pull a veil of darkness across our eyes that blinds us to the damage we're doing to others.

In part, this is why so many angry men or women don't "wake up" to the damage they've done to a home until the very walls of the family are falling down around them. The anger they have spewed out at members of their family has doubled back and blinded them to God's love and that of others.

Walking consistently in darkness prevents us from being lovingly sensitive toward others. It also kills any interest we have in studying God's Word and puts an icy chill on our desire to pray. Further, it robs us of any desire to please and honor Him or to experience His joy, contentment, and peace.

I've met a number of people who, after years of attending church and seeking God, have still not found peace. And after getting to know them better, the major reason for their failure in many cases is deep-seated anger.[5] They are unwilling to forgive or seek forgiveness, and as a result they hide pockets of darkness inside their lives—black holes in their souls that can expand throughout the years.

Anger does tremendous damage to a person physically and spiritually—and that's not all. It also goes to the emotional heart of a relationship and can bury any feelings of warmth or attachment in its icy darkness as well.

How can we tell that anger has begun to attack our relationship, pushing it into darkness? Our loved ones will begin to withdraw from us on every level—physical, emotional, and spiritual. That withdrawal is something I call a *closed spirit*. Left unchecked, this spirit can drain every bit of sparkle and vitality out of our families and leave them empty, wounded, and alone.

Recognizing a Person's Spirit

Let me get more specific about what I mean about a person's "spirit." It can be explained this way. When you meet someone for the first time, you interact with him on three levels—first with your spirit, then with your soul, and finally with your body.

Imagine with me that I walk up to a person at one of our seminars and meet him for the first time. Before ever we spoke a word, the first thing that would "touch" would be our *spirit*. I'm defining the "spirit" of a person as the innermost, intangible part of our being that tells us if there is any natural connection or friction between us. It's also that part of us that relates to God at times when words aren't enough.

Next, is the *soul* (the Greek word for soul is "psyche"). The soul is made up of three inseparable parts: the intellect, the will, and the emotions. When we communicate with a person, we engage at all three of these levels. For example, with the person I met at the seminar, we would no doubt exchange words when we meet. Later, if we come to know each other better, we would exchange ideas or even dreams. In that way, our "souls" would have touched or interacted.[6]

If our relationship entered the third level, and if it were appropriate, we could physically touch. For example, you and I would probably shake hands if we met for the first time. Now we've had a complete relationship—body, soul, and spirit. Granted, at this point it's a shallow relationship, but at least it has all the elements of a "total" relationship.

In our seminar, I use my hand to illustrate the open and closed spirit concept. To make sure you understand this principle, hold out your own hand right now.

Look at the palm of your hand, with the fingers spread wide apart. Let's say that the fingers wiggling around freely are the spirit of a person. They're the first thing to reach out and touch others. The semicircular ridge where the fingers meet the palm of the hand could represent the soul where people meet intellectually. And the very center of the palm could stand for the body.

When you are happy and all is well in your relationship with your mate, child, or friend, those fingers are wiggling and happy. The palm is open and exposed—ready to reach out and even to lovingly hold someone else's hand. An open hand could have represented the woman whose story we told at the beginning of this chapter. When she first married, she was open and eager for love.

If I offend a person or provoke him to anger, however, that open hand can begin to close. Take time to give yourself a living object lesson. Close your hand slowly and notice what happens. The spirit begins to close over the soul and the body. If it is allowed to tighten up all the way, what do you have? A closed fist —the world-wide symbol of anger and defiance. In short, you have what that man had when he called me in the middle of the night—a wife who was so deeply hurt and so "closed" to him that she lashed back with the force of a rock-hard fist.

As long as everything is healthy in a relationship, the hand is open, the fingers wiggling and happy. The spirit is open and responsive. But hurtful words and actions—allowed to grow into a bitter spirit—can one day lead to our being shut out of someone's life completely.

How Do We Close a Person's Spirit?

While there are probably hundreds of ways to offend someone—and close his or her spirit—we consistently see several that top the list. To repeat just a few, we can close a person's spirit by—

- Speaking harsh words
- Belittling a person's opinions
- Being unwilling to admit that we're wrong
- Taking a person for granted
- Making jokes or sarcastic comments at the other person's expense
- Not trusting a person
- Forcing a person to do something he's uncomfortable with
- Being rude to that person in front of others
- Ignoring a person's genuine needs as unimportant or not nearly as valuable as our own

That's just a sample of the "hit list" of actions that can close a person's spirit.[7] Our loved ones could probably make up their own list. We may not even be aware of what we do to deposit anger into their lives. When it comes to relationships, an important rule of thumb is, *whatever dishonors another person usually closes his spirit.*

While it wasn't my intended goal, I got an early start in closing Norma's spirit. When we were first married, I spoke at a number of youth groups. We were still in college, and we had no children, so Norma always went along with me to these meetings.

I thought I was quite funny at the time, and I would crack jokes at Norma's expense, totally unaware of how it was affecting her spirit. I would say things like, "Oh, it sure is great being married to Norma. She treats me just like a god! Every morning she serves me burnt offerings."

That would get big laughs. So then I'd follow up with something like, "Being married to Norma is just like being married to an angel—she's always up in the air harping about something and she never has an earthly thing to wear!"

And if I was really on a roll, I could always tell the kids about the time I pulled up to the airport with Norma and a sky cap asked, "Can I help you with your bag?" And I said, "No, thanks, she can walk." Later, in the car, you can guess what would happen.

Norma would often say, "I really didn't appreciate your jokes, Gary." To which I'd impatiently wave my hand, and say, "Oh, lighten up. You're *sooooo* sensitive!" I didn't realize it at the time, but each sarcastic comment was beginning to close her spirit to me.

Once again, part of the problem lies with the differences between men and women. Men are usually not aware that God has created most women with a highly sensitive spirit to sarcasm and criticism. I know I wasn't aware of this very important natural difference—particularly during that first important year of marriage.

My Own Valentine's Day Massacre

Six months or so after our wedding, Valentine's Day rolled around. It was our first Valentine's Day as a married couple and Norma had spent hours preparing a fancy meal just for me. In her mind as she was laboring over a hot stove, she was thinking thoughts like . . .

"It's Valentine's Day, and my new husband is going to be coming through the door any minute. He'll have a romantic card for me, and then we'll enjoy a memorable time together!"

What I did was certainly memorable—but it produced the kind of memory I'd like to forget. I called at two o'clock in the afternoon and said "Hon', I forgot to tell you something this morning. I've got a basketball game I'm going to play in tonight."

I could sense the surprise in her voice as she responded,

"But this is Valentine's Day!"

"I know, I know, but this game is *really* important."

Then Norma said,

"But I've already made this special dinner, and I've got the new tablecloth on, and candles set out, and . . . and . . ."

"Norma, I have to go to this game. I gave some of the guys my *word* that I'd be there." (Which meant that I wasn't about to embarrass myself by calling up my friends and telling them I had to stay home with my wife instead of playing basketball.)

For a long time, there was only silence on the other end of the phone. Although I'm ashamed of it now, do you know what I thought at the time? *Oh, no. I have a strong-willed woman on my hands!* I mistook a closing spirit for a strong will.

Right then I decided I might as well take advantage of this tailor-made opportunity to straighten her out. So, in a controlled, but firm, voice, I said, "Now, Norma, you know that I'm going into the ministry, *right*? One of the very important things that the Bible says is the wife should submit to her husband . . . ."

I'm sure you know how well my lecture went over. Her spirit began to close on me that very moment because of my total insensitivity—only I didn't realize it at the time. I was so blinded by my own self-interest, I couldn't see the negative writing on the walls of her life, though I would one day be forced to read it.

Bit by bit, month by month, I did more and more of these "little," insensitive things until I knocked the sparkle right out of her precious eyes. It's difficult for me, even after all these years, to think about how unaware I was of her spirit—and how insensitive and wrong I was.

The tragedy is, the more a man steps on the spirit of his wife, the more resistant she becomes toward him. The more resistant she becomes to him, the more he closes his spirit toward her. Soon, you have a vicious circle of two people in the same home who have made a public vow to love each other—now living under a private pledge to have a closed fist, not an open hand. As

I close my spirit to another person, what happens? It closes up my soul and my body as well.

"But how do I know that I'm actually closing someone's spirit?" The state of a child's spirit is the easiest to recognize, because children are not as practiced at hiding their real emotions. When children become closed to us in their souls, they disagree with everything we say, lose their desire to be "with the family," and seem to love to argue. Physically, they stop touching us, or they even resist our touch under any and all circumstances. They may even turn their backs on us when they see us.

To us, our remark may mean nothing. We may not even remember it. To us, our words may seem as light as a pebble. If I dropped a pebble on my spouse's or child's foot, I might think it should bounce right off without their notice. But for our loved ones, what is a "pebble" to us might be a ten-pound weight. And we just dropped it right on their barefoot toes!

Common Marks of a Closed Spirit

Because it's difficult for many of us to recognize when we've closed a family member's spirit, it's worth taking a moment to learn four common warning signs.

Warning sign number one *is a feeling of tension between you that you can't explain away.* That may be the spirit closing.

Warning sign number two *is an argumentative attitude.* They may resist discussing just about anything. They might avoid you, never ask for your advice, or criticize you for little or no reason. Before long, you can say the moon comes up at night and the sun in the day, and they'll find a way to disagree.

Some of us have worked for a boss who has deeply offended us. We know what it's like to disagree with anything he says—even before he says anything! If I have my spirit closed toward someone, I can have negative thoughts whenever I see that person.

The same thing happens when you step on the spirit of your children. Typically, they become resistant. It's the basic attitude of a persistently strong-willed child. Almost all toddlers (and most other kids of various ages) can go through "stages" of being strong-willed. If you win the battle early, then you can avoid facing many battles later in life.[8]

There is a major difference, though, in a child who is going through the normal "stages" of challenging mom and dad, and one who is retaliating out of anger by being stubborn or "resistant." You can tell a closed-fist child to take the trash out, and he won't be "typically" slow about it—he'll be blatantly defiant. "No, I'm *not* going to do it. You do it yourself or make someone else do it."

Warning sign number three *is a loss of physical intimacy.* Hugs and kisses? Forget it; your loved one probably won't want to get within a block of you. Almost all children go through times when "hugging" mom and dad isn't "cool" (or "hot," or "rad"). But even during these times, if parents are persistent and creative, they can fill up their child's "touch" bank with quick hugs and playful wrestling (with the guys). If, on the other hand, his or her spirit is closed to you, it'll be like an armed guard in front of the bank!

Close a spouse's spirit, and watch the romantic feelings all but evaporate. I've had a number of women tell me that emotionally they felt like prostitutes when their spirit was closed to their husbands and they were involved sexually anyway.

I've heard husbands growl, "That woman is totally uninterested or unresponsive!" Yet he may be the primary cause of her low level of sexual response as the one closing her spirit. Physical intimacy for a woman is spirit, soul, and body, not just body alone. All three levels have to be interrelated, otherwise any sexual response, for both men and women, is, at best, mechanical and, at worst, dysfunctional.

Warning sign number four is *negative nonverbal signals.* If a person's spirit is closing toward you, his facial expressions may even be more negative than his words. Physically, he may pull away from you, leave the door to his room shut consistently for "privacy," or even turn his back on you in the middle of a conversation. If your children resent being at home—especially being alone with you—that too may be a sign of a closed spirit.

A Window of Hope

My purpose in writing about a closed spirit is not to heap guilt on spouses or parents who may find themselves battling a fist rather than an opened palm. It is, rather, to give people hope. As I have tried to share in detail, things I've done to both my wife and children have closed their spirits to me for a short time, but the key to maintaining strong relationships over the years is to be able to reopen a loved one's closed spirit. It reminds me of what I had to do with my oldest son, Greg, when he was just a young boy.

Five Attitudes That Can
Help to Open a Loved One's Heart

In my parenting book, *The Key to Your Child's Heart,* I tell about my son Greg when he was about five or six years old. At the time, I worked for a large Christian organization, and I was often on the phone with pastors across the country. This also meant that I would have to take calls at home from a number of Christian leaders at times, so I made a rule in our home that couldn't be violated—nobody screams when I'm on the phone!

One evening I was in my bedroom on a long-distance phone call to a distinguished senior pastor. Suddenly, my son, Greg, let out a blood-curdling scream from the bathroom. He came running into the bedroom, screaming so loudly that I couldn't hear the person on the other end of the line.

"Hush!" I signaled to him emphatically, putting my hand over the mouthpiece of the phone, "Can't you see I'm on the phone?"

But Greg continued screaming, so I quickly ended my phone conversation, telling the person I'd have to call him back later.

When I hung up the phone, I grabbed Greg by the arm. "Why are you screaming and running around the house?" I demanded. "Couldn't you see I was on the phone?"

Without waiting for an answer, I hustled him down the hall and said, "You get into your bedroom right now." Still crying, Greg hurried into his room. Once we were inside, I picked up the little ruler that the kids had all helped to decorate (they affectionately named it the "teacher"). For breaking my inviolate rule, I swatted him on the bottom.

It was our practice after a spanking to hold the child and hug away any resentment, but this time, something took place that startled me.

"Come here so I can hug you," I said.

"No," he said, still crying, and the look in his eyes said, "I hate you." He backed away from me to let me know that he didn't want me to touch him at all.

Then after all that had happened, it hit me.

"Greg, why were you crying?"

With his little voice heaving with his sobs, he said, "I fell in the bathroom and hurt my ear and when you pushed me on the bed, I hurt it again."

He was hurt. That's why he was crying! Why hadn't I asked him earlier? Now I not only felt awful, I also felt like a child abuser. I knew I had closed Greg's spirit tightly at that moment, and if I didn't do something, it could leave an emotional scar on our relationship.

Convicted to my very heart, I got down on my knees.

"Greggy," I said in the softest voice I could. "I'm so sorry that I didn't ask you what was wrong or why you were screaming. You didn't deserve a spanking. I'm the one that deserves to be spanked." I held out the little stick to him, but he dropped it and backed up. It was obvious that he still didn't want any part of me.

So I said, "Greg, I was so wrong. Maybe you can't do it right now, but I wonder if you could forgive me? Would you?" Then it was as if his little heart melted, and he rushed into my arms. I fell back onto the bed with him in my arms and just held him tightly as his sobs slowly turned into regular breathing.

After a long time, I asked him again to be sure, "Greg, are you sure you've forgiven Daddy?"

He just patted me and said, "Oh, Daddy, we all make mistakes."

Do you know what that told me about Greg? It told me that Greg was opening his spirit to me. He was touching me. We were talking. His feelings were coming back. His body, soul, and spirit were reopening.

What was happening between us as we held each other was the result of five attitudes that work together to help open the spirit of a person. Let me state clearly, *these are not steps.* You can't mechanically go down the list and expect to wipe away every hurt or draw out all the anger in a relationship. With Greg, it took only a half-hour to reopen his spirit and put us back into harmony. With Norma, it took almost two years of consistently applying these attitudes to reverse all the closing of her spirit I had done.

The important thing is not the time it takes, but the decision and commitment to do whatever it takes to come back into harmony with a person *to release as much anger as possible.* For years now, I have practiced these same attitudes with my wife and each of my children. They have been a tremendous help in making sure anger is drained out of our home each day. I know they can be an encouragement in your home as well.

Five Attitudes to Reopen a Person's Spirit

1. Become soft and tender with the person

Proverbs says, "A gentle answer turns away wrath" (Proverbs 15:1). My whole problem with Greg started when I became harsh and unreasoning. Things began to turn around when my tone of voice softened along with my spirit. My attitude, nonverbals, and voice said I cared about him. Sometimes softness alone can open a person's spirit. That's the whole message of Chapter 5.

2. Understand, as much as possible, what the other person has gone through (remember, listen to what is said; do not react to the words used)

I would have cried if I had fallen in the bathtub, too. Then to get a spanking on top of that? So I showed Greg by my words, as best I could, that I understood what he felt. I talked with him about how awful it must have been, all the time being careful not to "react" to something he said defensively.

3. Acknowledge that the person is hurting, and be sure to admit any wrong in provoking anger

"Greg," I said, "I was so wrong." As a parent (or a spouse), it can be very hard to say those words at times, but as it did with Greg, it can work wonders. Admitting we are wrong (when we clearly are) is like drilling a hole in our loved one's "anger bucket" and allowing that unhealthy emotion to drain away. Once they hear us admit it, the anger has a way to escape from their lives.

Sometimes we may not think we are wrong, but our attitude might be. Or, it may be the way we've done something that's offensive. If my attitude is harsh and angry when I tell my wife about a legitimate problem, I'm still wrong. ". . . Man's anger (or that of a woman) does not bring about the righteous life that God desires" (James 1:20). Stopping short of admitting we were wrong leaves a dangerous gap between you and your child or mate that may not mend quickly—or at all.

4. Touch the other person gently

If you step on your mate's spirit at ten o'clock at night (or in the morning) and then you get into bed and expect to be amorous, what's likely to happen? Your spouse may move way over to the other side of the bed. That's when you'll hear that she has a headache, it's the wrong year, or she just doesn't want to be touched. The nonverbal message, "No touchie the toes," may mean, "My spirit is closing to you."

If you try to touch someone with a closed spirit, you will find out just how deep the hurt is. If a woman has only been touched in anger or to meet her husband's sexual needs, she may resent *any* touch and pull away, or be stiff and unbending. But persistent softness—expressed in meaningful touches apart from any demands for sex—can go a long way toward draining anger and negative feelings from a relationship.

5. Seek forgiveness—and wait for a response

Say something like, "Could you forgive me? I've disappointed you so many times. I know I don't deserve to be forgiven, but could you try?" or "I don't want you all tied up in knots, not responding to me at all. I know I have a million miles to go before I get everything together in my life, but I love you very much, and I ask you to forgive me. Will you forgive me?"

Try to get a positive response from the person before you quit, but if you need to, start with the first loving attitude of being soft and work your way back down to forgiveness again. Remember, too, *don't just respond to your loved one's words.* In the heat of battle, or if you've deeply hurt someone, that person may say something in retaliation to hurt you: "That's right," they might respond. "You *don't* deserve to be forgiven. I really don't know how I live with you when you mess up so often."

For many people, men in particular, hearing words that may hit below the belt can set off a defensive lecture—or even be an invitation to another round of angry retaliation. But those men and women who are wise enough to reopen a person's spirit have to learn to listen beyond the words to the hurt feelings behind the words.

There have been times when I felt something Norma said to me was unfair, even though I was trying to be soft and ask her to forgive me. Perhaps she misinterpreted my motives or even questioned my character in the process, but when you're asking another person to forgive you, it's not the time to get into a lecture on the precise wording of the problem. Your focus should be on draining away the anger and not on compounding it.

The senior pastor at our home church is an exceptional individual. One of the many things we've learned from Darryl DelHousaye is a biblical admonition on dealing with anger. I've found it to be universally true in relationships. Time and again, Darryl has said from the pulpit, concerning anger and the need for forgiveness, "Biblically, the stronger person always initiates the peace." Are you willing to be the "strong" one who seeks to set things right in a relationship? Sometimes it takes a strong act of the will not to react to someone's words. Remember—in most cases it was hasty reactions that helped to close that person's spirit in the first place.

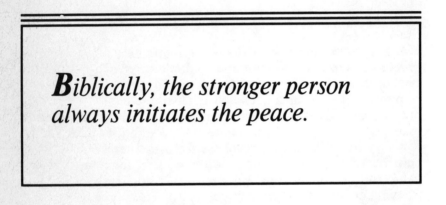

*B*iblically, the stronger person always initiates the peace.

Untying Our Own Knots

There is an important reason why forgiveness plays such a pivotal part in opening a person's spirit. It has to do with the very way the Bible defines the word. In the original biblical language, remember, the word for forgiveness means "to release, set free, to untie."

With that picture in mind, when we say or do something offensive to other people, we are actually helping, emotionally and spiritually, to tie them in knots. Perhaps what we've done has come as the result of knots someone else has left in our lives.

Do you know why most "difficult" people are so ill-natured, people who don't like themselves, who are resentful, or who feel rejected? Such people battle forgiving others—or feeling forgiven themselves. The way they tell us that they're tied up is through their negative, obnoxious actions. That's one reason why the

Scriptures say we are to love our enemies. Their negative reactions are warning signals that their lives are tied up in knots.

What about my own knots, though? someone may be thinking. *How can I get the knots out of another person's life when I'm all tied up myself?* In the Lord's Prayer, Christ answers this important question.

If we could paraphrase a few verses, using the literal definition of forgiveness, it could read like this: "If you are willing to untie the knots of the one who offended you, then God will untie your own knots (forgive you). If you refuse to untie their knotted lives, then God won't untie yours." One major reason why forgiveness is so necessary is that anger blocks the working of God's spirit.

Can you see now that leaving someone angry is allowing them to be in "darkness" and tied up in "knots"? Not only are we damaging a person emotionally when we provoke anger in them, but we are also cutting them off from God's light. There is, however, an antidote to unhealthy anger.

If we are attaching value and honor to the people around us, then we will do our best never to do anything that ties them up in knots. If we do, we will try to untie them. "Do not let the sun go down on your anger" (Ephesians 4:26 RSV).

In Chapters 13 and 15, we'll share specifically about untying the knots that may be in your life. For now, though, keeping harmony in a home comes from understanding the attitudes that can reopen a loved one's life and love to us.

Never . . . Never Give Up

There is one final question we must raise. What if we try our best, and they still don't respond?

Gently persist . . . gently persist . . . gently, lovingly persist.

Near the end of his life, Winston Churchill was asked to give a commencement speech at a noted university in England. His car arrived late, and the jam-packed crowd suddenly hushed as one of the greatest men in British history made his way slowly, painfully to the podium.

Churchill's speech lasted less than two minutes—but it drew a standing ovation. It comprised only twelve words, but it has inspired decades of men and women ever since. What he said is the best advice I can give you when it comes to being persistent in love to open a spouse's or child's spirit. What did he say?

With his deep, gruff, resonating voice, he said, "Never give up. . . Never, never, give up. . . Never, never, never give up."

End of speech, but not the end of the message. If the man who called me at midnight had given up on being persistent in love, he would have sent a wife and family away tied up in knots and still in darkness.

I'm not sure if I have ever heard a more hostile woman than the one I called that morning. Yet a little less than a year later, she called me back and said, "Gary, I just wanted you to know that I'm back together with my husband. . . ."

I'll have to admit I was floored when I received her call. From every human angle, their relationship was dead in the water that fateful evening when she locked her husband out of the house. Obviously she had thought the same thing.

"A year ago," she said, "if you had even *suggested* that there was a possibility we would be back together—that I would even *like* him, much less love him again—I wouldn't have believed you. The amazing thing," she continued, "is that I do love him again. I actually want to be around him. That fascinates me all by itself. . . ."

What happened to bring about such a change? Because this man recognized that he had let anger ruin his home—and learned how to drain it out of his wife's life—he reopened her spirit, and he did one thing more. His commitment to allow God to change him and his attitude toward his family made him never, never give up—even when she said she hated him and never wanted to see him again.

If I had given up any one of a hundred times of working to get the anger out of Norma or one of my children's lives, I probably wouldn't be writing this book now—or enjoying the strong relationships we have at home. What I and my friend learned about opening a person's spirit can work for you too—as it has in my family—to help us all avoid a major destroyer of families.

Now we head into one of my favorite subjects: the tremendous value of a man. For God has given a man exactly what he needs to be a great lover and leader of his home. We men come to the marriage relationship equipped to contribute four essential ingredients that lie at the heart of a rock-solid relationship. Let's discover what those ingredients are.

7

The Tremendous Value of a Man

Just picture the scene. Norma and I are getting ready to begin one of our evening marriage encounter groups—an important part of the early work we did on a church staff. Everyone has been walking around, smiling, drinking coffee, catching up on small talk. Now they're all settling comfortably into the chairs we've arranged around the living room. Then, suddenly, the peaceful atmosphere is shattered.

With a bang, the front screen door swings open. In walks one of the couples from the group. The husband darts ahead of his wife and takes over the couch. Without a word, he crosses his arms and glares at everybody. His wife's eyes are red and puffy, and she walks right past him and sits down across the room, next to one of the other wives.

Only a few seconds had passed, and the evening had gone from easygoing to explosive! Since I was the leader of the group, I decided to get started, thinking that would help.

I opened with a prayer, then looked at the man again. He was still sitting with his arms tightly crossed, looking like Mount St. Helens just before it erupted. Thinking it might relieve some of the tension, I started off with him.

"How's it going this week?" I asked.

"*Terrible!*" he snarled.

"Okay," I said. "What's so terrible?"

"If you really want to know," he replied, leaning forward in his chair and looking me right in the eye, "I've been thinking about getting out of this marriage group.

"No—I'll tell you what," he continued, raising his volume level up a notch, "I've got a better idea. What I'm really thinking about is getting out of my marriage! I *can't stand* that woman over there, and I don't know if I can live with her any longer." His words ripped through the air as he sat back in his chair, a look of defiance on his face.

It was interesting to see what happened the instant he stopped talking. All the women immediately glared at him, and then went over to comfort his wife, and every man in the room instantly did the same thing, only for him. We all looked at each other and thought, *What do we do now?*

As the leader of the group, I knew I had to take charge, so I said, "Why don't we close in prayer?" And that's exactly what I did. It was probably the shortest marriage group meeting on record. As everyone filed into the kitchen, I was able to pull the man aside and asked, "Listen, why don't we get together for lunch tomorrow before you do something drastic?"

Reluctantly, he agreed.

The next day, as we talked at a restaurant downtown, we both discovered something fascinating. In fact, it's something I've used to strengthen my own marriage and have shared with hundreds of men since.

Self-Inflicted Wounds in a Relationship

"Why do you want to leave your wife? What bothers you the most about her?" I asked.

"Gary, there isn't enough time over lunch for me to tell you everything that gripes me. It'd take all afternoon!"

"Just try to hit the high points then," I said. In a few minutes, he had shared five things about her that were particularly irritating.

"She's a sloppy housekeeper . . . she's on the phone all the time . . . she's with her mother constantly . . . she won't take any trips with me . . . she never initiates when it comes to sex."

As the list piled up, his attitude became harder and harder. I threw up a quick prayer for wisdom and then I did something I'd never done before. I began by taking each one of his "gripes" in order and asking him specific questions about them. Questions like: "When it comes to her housekeeping, do you ever encourage her? For instance, do you ever praise her for the good things she does around the house?"

"No," he replied. "She never *does* anything good around the house for me to compliment."

"At least give me an example of what you might say to her when her housekeeping skills don't measure up to where you want them," I went on.

"Well," he said, his tone softening just a little, "the other day I got up and started vacuuming the house at six o'clock in the morning. When I started down the hallway toward our bedroom, she got out of bed and said 'What are you doing?' and I said, 'I'm sick and tired of living in this pig pen! We're cleaning up this place, and we're doing it *now!*'"

"Do you think that motivates her to keep the house clean?" I asked.

"No, I guess it doesn't. But that still doesn't solve the problem of her being a slob," he retorted. Ignoring his barbs, I continued through his list, asking questions.

"After work and on weekends, how much time do you spend actually talking to your wife about something important to her?"

"Well, frankly there's not a lot of time left over in my week. I've got a crushing schedule at the office. I play racquetball three days a week, and then we have to fit in *your* group which takes another night," he said, making sure I knew how much effort he was expending just to be in the group. "And I've got to do something to relax on the weekends, so I usually play golf with some of the guys from work. . . ."

"Do you spend any time talking to her during dinner?" I asked.

Reluctantly he replied, "I usually watch television during dinner. Basically, that's the only time I have to catch the news. But Gary, you've got to understand. In my line of work it's crucial for me to know what's going on, nationally and internationally, to see how it might affect my business."

I said, "Okay, the news may be important, but do you spend *any* time with her during the week, just the two of you, talking together about your lives? About what's important to her, not just your business?"

"No," he said in an emotionless voice, "not really."

I said, "Then it's no wonder she's on the phone day and night and always over at her mother's. A woman comes equipped with a tremendous need for meaningful communication—particularly with her husband. If that need is blocked, she'll find someone else to talk to."

"Oh," he said, a series of tiny lights beginning to switch on inside his mind, "I never thought of it that way."

"You've got your own company now, but in the past have you ever worked for a guy who was very critical?" I asked.

"You bet I have," he said, without pausing even a moment to think about it.

"I had one boss I really hated. He was the kind of guy who couldn't *wait* to come into my office to criticize me. He'd point out anything that was going wrong or even could go wrong in my department. Then he'd yell at me to 'Shape up! Do this! Do that!' After his tirade in front of all the other people I worked with, he'd go back in his office and drink coffee while I worked my head off."

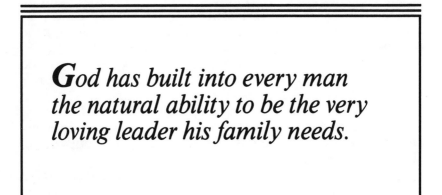

*G*od has built into every man the natural ability to be the very loving leader his family needs.

I said, "How did that make you feel?"

"How did it make me *feel?* I hated working with him," he answered. "I couldn't wait until the end of the day just to get away from him."

"Would you like to go on a vacation with him?" I asked.

"A *vacation?* Are you kidding?" he said incredulously. "That'd be the *last* thing I'd want to do."

I said, "Don, do you realize that you're treating your wife the same way that boss treated you?"

His eyes widened, and he sat straight up in his chair as he took in what I said.

"It's no wonder your wife doesn't want to go on a trip with you, or even to respond to you physically. The way you've been treating her, it's as if she's living night and day with your former boss."

After a long silence, he grudgingly said, "You've got a point there."

We went through all five areas he'd mentioned and made an amazing discovery. With each and every problem he had with his wife, he was at least partially responsible for creating the very attitudes and actions that were so irritating to him.

"What do I do now?" he asked, plaintively.

It's not that this man's negative contributions to his marriage in any way justified his wife's negative behavior, but in many ways, his behavior helped support her actions. Basically, he had no idea he was adding to the very things he didn't want to see in his home. Now that he realized it, he didn't know how to begin to change.

Would you describe this man as a lover? Not really. Would you describe him as a nurturer? Not likely. Could he (and did he) become both? Definitely.

Unlocking a Man's Natural Strength

I am convinced that most men, if they have a plan and know what to do, are willing to take the steps to build a loving, lasting relationship.[1] The problem is that the average man doesn't know intuitively what it takes to do so—nor does he realize the incredible benefits that a strong relationship at home brings to nearly every area of his life.[2]

Remember the women's "built-in marriage manual" we talked about in Chapter 4? In that chapter, we shared how by nature, God seems to equip a woman from birth with important skills a man tends to lack. In part, that is the reason for the special title she bears as a man's "completer" and "helper" (Genesis 2:18).

For some people, a woman's natural edge in relationships can be used as ammunition for blasting men and a man's place in the home. Some people have even read some of my earlier books and felt that I was jumping on the "men-bashing" bandwagon. However, I'd like to set the record straight.

While it is true a man doesn't speak as many words or may not be as naturally sensitive as a woman, that doesn't mean he is incapable of being a great lover in the home. In fact, it seems that *God has built into every man the natural ability to be the very loving leader his family needs.*

Saying that God has designed a man to be the lover in a home may sound a bit strange after all we've said about a man's conquering, logical, fact-driven nature, but that very nature is the foundation for my conviction.

Why? Because the kind of love that lasts, the kind that can grow and thrive apart from feelings, is the kind that comes from a decision. And as I mentioned in Chapter 3, *love*—stripped to its core—is just that, *a factual decision that doesn't have to depend on our feelings*.

There are times in life when we may not feel like doing something that's important, but we still need to do it. We need to give our two-year-old the medicine she needs when she flatly refuses to take it. Or we may have to stay up late to finish the report that has to be done on time—no matter how it bends our schedule or robs us of sleep. Or perhaps it's getting up an hour early each day to exercise and spend time in the Word and in prayer. Whatever the situation, there are times when all our "natural" instincts may say "no," but God's Word or another person's best interest demands we say "yes."

When it comes to family relationships, that same hard-driving, conquering nature that can cause a man to get ahead in his profession, can cause one of two results at home. In many cases, it can create emotional strain and tension if a man tries to blast through his family relationships like so many projects at work. Take that same drive and harness it by giving a man a specific plan of action for the home—and it can be the driving force to bring about the very relationship a woman longs for.

If the truth be known, that man in my marriage group came into his marriage with tremendous *liabilities*. He didn't have a loving father as a child, and the two communication skills his parents modeled for him were anger and silence. Yet, though he didn't know it at the time, in spite of the poor example he'd grown up with, he still possessed a God-given *ability* on which he could draw—anytime—to develop a strong marriage. Namely, once he knew what it took to have a fulfilling relationship, he could tap into his natural drive and desire to "win" and use it to strengthen his marriage.

It's hard for many women to understand how in an intimate relationship, a man is often more motivated to communicate if he puts facts in front of feelings. Normally, a woman will feel something, and then do it. For example, she'll feel an emotional need for communication, and then seek out her husband to meet that need. That's simply not the case with most men.

Usually a man is not driven by an emotional need to relate. Rather, he'll be much more motivated to do something relational (like spending a half-hour in conversation) once he's made a factual decision that it's right. For a man, actions are primarily what dictate feelings, not the reverse.

In large part, I feel that a man's unique ability to blend fact and feeling is a major gift God has given him in order to carry out his responsibility of being the loving leader in a home. When a man is given the right information, told what is right to do and how to do it, he can draw on his natural force of will to make a decision that *stays* while his feelings may come and go.

A Biblical Blueprint for Loving Leadership in a Home

For a man, the first place he should check when it comes to building a strong family is a blueprint found in Ephesians 5. In this important chapter, the man is called to be the "head" of his wife—the primary lover—just as Christ is the head of the church and the lover of the church.

Nowhere does it say that a man is to "lord it over" his wife. In fact, Christ specifically commands that "lording it over" another person has no place in a Christian's relationships. Rather, the Scriptures tell me I am to love my wife as Jesus loves His church.

How did Christ lead in love? By serving, by committing Himself to our best interest, and by doing so regardless of the cost. The greatest among us are simply following a pattern Christ set down—namely serving those He loved and for whom He laid down His life.

Yet let's take the command for a man to be a loving leader in the home, and move it down to the shoe-leather level. What does it mean to be the "leader" in a home?

When it comes to "leadership" and headship in the home, one very specific guideline is found in verses 28–29, ". . . husbands ought to love their wives, as their own bodies . . . . (for) no one ever hated his own body, but he *feeds* and *cares* for it, just as Christ also does the church" (emphasis added).

If we are following the biblical pattern for family leadership, we men are to nurture and cherish our wives (and children). We do so just as we nurture and cherish our own bodies—and as Christ nurtures and cherishes the church.

When a husband makes that first important decision to truly honor those entrusted to him, he takes the first step toward being the loving *nurturer* God meant him to be. As a result he can see his relationship begin to blossom before his eyes and grow.

Growing a Strong Marriage

What does it actually mean to "nurture" one's wife?

The Greek word for "nurturer" means "husbandman."[3] For those of us who haven't grown up on a farm, that's a tiller of the soil, a professional gardener. A nurturer is one who helps things grow, who provides a "greenhouse" atmosphere where the plants are shielded and protected.

In short, that's what I'm called to be as a husband. Like the top gardener at your local nursery, I am responsible for understanding what ingredients cause my marriage to grow and flower—and then for providing them on a consistent basis. The psalmist puts it this way. "Blessed are all who fear the Lord. . . . Your wife shall be like a fruitful vine within your house; your sons like olive shoots around your table . . ." (Psalm 128:3).

Can you imagine what would happen if that gardener at your local nursery went by guesswork when it came to caring for his plants? No wonder in many marriages we see a "Under New Management" or "Gone Out of Business" sign up in the front yard. No less skill is required of the "head" of a marriage. He is called to be a skilled nurseryman, a caretaker of sorts. He is to be the first one to recognize and supply the ingredients needed for growth and well-being in the family and the first to spot and pull any weeds that threaten to do it harm.

In short, *my role as a "nurturer" is to be a fact-finder.* I should interview each member of my family with my fact-finder mind to see what needs should be met that day and then discover how best to meet them. When I do, I nurture, cover and protect them—and get the privilege of watching them grow. In my own life, one word picture has helped to cement this concept of nurturing in my memory.

A Man Has a Natural,
Relational "Green Thumb"

After we bought our first little home in Rockford, Illinois, I decided to plant a victory garden. I had heard that the ashes from burned leaves helped the soil, so I gathered a huge pile of leaves from all over the yard. My leaf pile burned all night long, and that's not all. At one point the wind shifted and I nearly burned down my neighbor's garage as well.

Barely escaping disaster, the next day I spread out all the ashes in the back part of the yard where I was planning my garden. I didn't really know what I was doing, but it looked great! The earth was dark and moist, and a few weeks later, the results were even better than I expected. Whatever we planted came up looking like the pictures on the seed packet covers.

Everything grew. In fact, the pumpkins became so enthusiastic about the soil that they grew along the fence and up into a tree and hung down everywhere like Christmas ornaments. After my one experience of gardening in Rockford, I felt that I was gifted with a permanently green thumb. However, one day I discovered that the green on my thumb was disappearing ink.

We had moved a thousand miles away, and I decided to unleash my gardening talents on the Lone Star state. From the first spade of soil I turned, I could tell things were going to be different in Waco, Texas. There the ground was a white, rocky, clayish dirt, not the deep brown I had been used to in Rockford.

Without consulting any of the local nurserymen or gardening books, I simply made the decision that what the soil must need was additional fertilizer. With that in mind, I went out and bought the biggest sack I could find with a label that said "For Gardens" on it. The picture on the sack looked just like the results I'd gotten in Rockford, so I figured this was exactly what I needed in Waco.

Spring came around, we put all the seed into the ground, and sure enough everything came up just like in the pictures. After a short time, the picture began to change radically. The beans started browning around the edge, the tomatoes were rotten in the middle, when we picked them, and our carrots were always spongy and wilted. It was obvious something was very wrong with this garden, but I didn't know exactly what to do.

Take Time to Talk to Your Garden . . .

At the time, I didn't realize that by dumping loads of fertilizer on soil that was already high in nitrogen, I was burning up my plants! Do you know what would have helped immeasurably, were it possible?

If only my garden could talk back to me, it could have let me know exactly what I was doing wrong—and what I could do to correct things. It may seem a little far-fetched, but I could say to my garden for example, "Good morning, down there, how are y'all doing?" And right off, the beans would speak up.

"How are we all doing down here? *We're dying!* That's how we're doing!"

"Come again?" I'd ask.

"We're dying down here! We're choking to death!"

"Hey, what's the problem?"

Then they'd say,

"Mr. Smalley, you know all those white things you poured around our roots? Well, now there are thousands of them, and they're killing us. Didn't you know how much nitrogen is in this soil already, and now you're dumping pounds of it all around us!"

I'd say, "No kidding? I didn't know I was hurting you. I never even thought to check the soil. What can I do to try to solve the problem?"

And they'd say, "Go down to the store and get some chemicals and neutralize this nitrogen. You've got to hurry, Mr. Smalley, we've only got a few days left!"

"Good idea! I'll take care of that." So I start to race off to the nursery when I notice my carrots, and I say to them, "Oh, look at your leaves, they're just wilting all over the place. Bless your pea-pickin' hearts!"

"Mr. Smalley," they cry out, "forget the peas. They're done for, but you can help us if while you're at the nursery, you pick up a nylon mesh to put over us to keep us cooler. Then we could really firm up."

"I never knew that!" I would say. "Listen, you sweet things you, I'll take care of everything, don't you worry."

If only I could have talked to my garden in Waco, I could have solved my green thumb problems in a few hours. Who knows? I could have even landed in a Miracle-Gro commercial. Unfortunately, my garden was for the birds—literally. Because I never took the time or had the wisdom to ask someone what the plants needed in my area, I ruined an entire summer's crop.

I suppose I could have taken a different approach to my "talking" garden. For example, I could have walked down early in the morning, taken one look, and said, "Hey, what's this mess? Look at all your leaves—they're browning out around the edges. Hey, you plants! Any more brown leaves on any of you and I'm going to jerk you up by the roots! Now shape up, all of you, and I mean *now!*"

Would my yelling at the plants have changed things around my garden? In actuality, I had caused much of the damage that my garden now displayed because I relied on wishing, not wisdom.

After almost twenty years of working with couples and families, I can testify that many husbands nurture the priceless relationships in their homes using the same principle that I employed in my gardens—*guesswork*. A husband often enters marriage with a picture of a great home in his mind, but relies on wishing, not hard work and wisdom, to see it come to reality. Unfortunately, when many men wake up to the damage they've done to their families, the summer's crop has almost been wasted and a bitter cold winter is fast setting in.

In short, that's why God calls the husband to be a wise "gardener" of his family. Each season of life, a man needs to prepare the soil of his family's lives, to protect them from the elements, and to mend the damage after any natural crisis. The better a man learns to be the nurturer in his home, the more it will look like the "picture" the Scriptures paint of a successful relationship. Wives and children, like the plants the psalmist talks about, reflect how well they've been gardened.

Going to a Plant for Lessons in Gardening

"Wait a minute," I can hear some men saying. "This nurturing business sounds like it puts all the responsibility on the man. What about the responsibility of a woman, or even the children, to make the home all it can be?"

Whenever I hear this argument, two things come to mind. First, it is true that a man is called to be the nurturer of his family, not a woman. In fact, the Scriptures never tell a woman to "love" her husband, but a man is specifically commanded to "love" his wife.

Throughout the Scriptures, a woman is pictured as the "responder" or reflector of her husband's and God's light. In the Song of Songs in the Old Testament, the bride of Solomon makes this important comment about their relationship, "Draw me after you, and let us run together!" (1:4, NASB).

Can you see the balance in this perspective? The man initiates the loving actions (drawing her after him); the woman responds (let us run together); and then the two of them grow together as a result. As we saw in Chapter 3, a woman's natural calling is to be a completer, a helper, a responder to his love. In addition, she is called to honor her husband (Romans 12:10; 1 Peter 3:1). When it comes to who wears the nurturing shoes in the family, biblically they come in men's sizes.

"But how can I know specifically what my wife needs, so that her life and our marriage blooms and grows?" you may ask. "I barely have time to finish everything I've got going at work. How am I going to learn all it takes to care for her in the way I should? Isn't that asking a lot?"

You're exactly right. It is asking a great deal to see that a marriage becomes successful. Without a doubt, a husband has a high calling in taking on the role of the nurturer in a home, but the task isn't impossible. In fact, it's far from it.

What are those nonnegotiable ingredients to a successful marriage? After years of counseling, researching, and interviewing couples throughout the world, it's apparent a healthy relationship needs at least four things.

As we've mentioned, by nature a woman tends to manifest these actions—and to desire them deeply. But if a husband understands these needs in the home (needs his wife and children have on an everyday basis), then makes the decision to apply them consistently in his marriage, it's almost impossible for healthy growth not to take place. What are these four nonnegotiable ingredients that can form a handbook for a committed nurturer—*man or woman?*

At the heart of "nurturing" our loved ones are providing . . .
    1) Deep-seated security
    2) Meaningful conversation
    3) Emotional/romantic times
    4) Positive physical touching

In almost all my books, I've talked about these four factors —and the only consistent power source that underlies each one. But as I speak, study, and talk to people across the country, my understanding of them deepens each year. These four needs are so essential that we'll take several chapters to highlight them all (and then two chapters at the end of the book in particular that talk about where we find the power to grow a love that lasts).

To begin with, let's take a look at the first ingredient in causing a husband, a wife, or child's life to bloom and grow. It's an ingredient that is so essential that with it, a family can experience fulfilling relationships. Without it, they often find nothing but frustration and constant bickering.

8

The First Aspect of Nurturing: Adding the Sunlight of Security to Your Relationships

In some counseling sessions, trying to get a couple to open up about the real issues they're struggling with is like trying to twist the lid off an old honey jar. When all else fails, there's a method that works every time. In fact, it's as effective as holding that honey jar under steaming, hot water.

All you have to do is invite God's little spies—their children —into the counseling session, and it's amazing how they can pop the lid off "hidden" problems in an instant. That's just what happened when Dr. Trent asked the young six-year-old daughter of one couple, "Honey, what makes you feel the worst when Mommy and Daddy argue?"

The little girl frowned and said in a small, hesitant voice, "It's when Daddy takes off his wedding ring and throws it away."

The husband quickly defended himself by saying that he didn't "actually" throw his ring away. Rather, it was only an unusual way of demonstrating his anger during a fight with his wife.

When this couple got into a heated argument, if he wanted to end the discussion he would take his wedding ring off and throw it across the room. As it pinged off the walls and rolled across the floor, the wife and his little girl would watch in silence. Later, someone would pick up the fallen ring and leave it on the counter. Eventually the husband would put it back on.

For this man, "throwing away" his wedding ring provided an immature emotional release from his frustration. For his wife and child, it caused a deep sense of insecurity and fear.

As the people who depended so much on him saw his ring go flying across the room, they saw their security level flying away as well. He didn't actually need to say the words that he was leaving. He let a flying gold band do the talking for him. Each time the ring flew through the air it shouted out, "If things don't go the way I want around here, I'll throw you right out of my life too."

Living Life on an Icy Street . . .

Have you ever endured an ice storm in your home town and then tried to walk down the street? It can be done but there's always the internal tension of knowing a terrible fall is right around the corner.

What many husbands and wives don't realize is that an absence of security in a relationship is like sentencing a person to live on an ice-covered sidewalk.

You're never free to truly relax in a home where insecurity has frozen the relationship in an icy state. It's impossible to enjoy a marriage when you're always fighting to keep your footing.

Unfortunately, in more and more homes across the country, it is always winter and never spring. There are months at a time when the cold January clouds of insecurity are never penetrated by the warm sunlight of security. Yet there is an antidote to living life under a dark cloud cover.

You can warm up your relationship in a dramatic way. In fact, you can actually do something *today* that is like turning the full force of a July sun right on your marriage. What is it? It's providing this first crucial aspect of nurturing our loved ones—unconditional security.

The Warmth to Thaw out a Relationship and Help It Grow

Security is like providing warm, invigorating sunlight to a plant. Leave a plant in the icy darkness of insecurity, and soon its leaves will wilt and turn brown. If a relationship has just been planted, the cold shadows of mistrust can keep any growth from ever sprouting above the surface. A plant must have sunlight if it's to ever be healthy and flourishing. In a marriage, the same thing is true.

Security results when a man and a woman say to each other, "You're so valuable to me that no matter what happens in life, I'm going to commit myself to you. You're so valuable, I'm going to spend the rest of my life proving to you my pledge to love you." In short, it's a reflection of the kind of security we have in our relationship with Christ. Look at Romans 8 for example:

"Who shall separate us from the love of Christ? . . . For I am convinced that neither death nor life, neither angels nor demons, neither the present nor the future . . . nor anything else in all creation will be able to separate us from the love of God that is in Christ Jesus our Lord" (Romans 8:35–39).

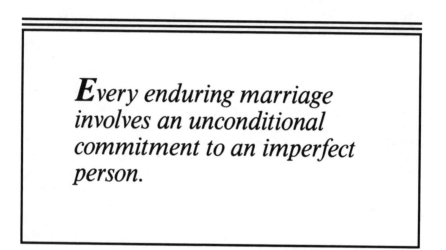

Every enduring marriage involves an unconditional commitment to an imperfect person.

God also goes to great lengths to assure us that the plans He has for us are grounded in His security and His protection. "'For I know the plans that I have for you,' declares the Lord, 'plans to prosper you and not to harm you, plans to give you a hope and a future'" (Jeremiah 29:11).

Now, that's security! And the better able we are to reflect the same level of security that we have in Christ to our loved ones, the more we bathe them in much needed sunlight. That goes for mothers who want to see their children feel confident in friend-ships and later in dating relationships. It's true for fathers who desire these same kids to do well in school and later in their professions. It's especially true for a husband or wife who want to live with the green leaves of a healthy marriage—not the brown leaves of a dying one.

Every enduring marriage involves an unconditional commitment to an imperfect person. This means we can gaze at each other's imperfections and say, "Those brown leaves do irritate me, but I'm going to find out what caused them, and see if I can help. No matter what shape you're in—I'll be around and help you grow." Without this kind of commitment, we're more likely to say, "I can't stand all these brown leaves. They've bothered me for years! That's it! I'm leaving."

If you're in a second marriage, I realize that talking about commitment "no matter what" can be an invitation to guilt feelings. Study after study exposes the long-term negative effects of insecurity that often follow a divorce. However, this still doesn't mean that genuine "security" is somehow out of reach in a remarriage situation.

Men and women who have, biblically and personally, dealt with their divorce and who have remarried have an equal or even greater need to build security in their present marriage. Like love, security is a decision we make on an everyday basis. (For those who may be struggling with guilt or fear from a past relationship, in Chapters 13 and 14 I'll look at ways God can use even something as traumatic as a divorce to make us more loving.)

For all of us, security is an essential prerequisite, not an emotional elective. Let's be even more specific in discussing how we can help our loved ones grow by providing the sunlight of security for their lives. There are at least three things that every man and woman can begin to do to build a secure marriage on an everyday basis.

They can start by 1) building their own "hallway of honor" in their home which in itself can help steer their mate or children away from the doorway of dishonor. Then they can 2) look to the Lord for the strength to make an unconditional commitment and sacrificial choices. Finally, 3) they can become students of their spouses' interests as a tangible way of expressing their commitment.

All are important ways to build security in a home, but the first has a dual benefit. It not only builds positive things into the relationship, it can also help to keep tremendous pain from the people we care about most.

1. A Hallway of Honor . . .

In the hallway of our patio-home, there is a plaque hanging on one wall that proclaims: "In assurance of my lifelong commitment. To Norma, Kari, Greg and Mike. Christmas 1976." Hardly a week goes by that I don't remind those four special people about those words and the commitment behind them.

I realize that words can be cheap. I've spoken with many hurting spouses and children who "believed" the words of commitment of a man or woman whose promises held as much weight as thin air. For them, their spouse walked out on the family leaving a doorway of shame, not a hallway of honor.

I fully realize the only things that will transfer the words of this plaque onto my spouse and children's hearts are my everyday actions and words over the years. Each time I match those words with my demonstrated commitment, I'm adding on to a "hallway of honoring acts" in my home. As a result, I'm leaving a daily legacy of love to my wife and children,[1] not a hurtful inheritance of emotional pain.

A marriage or family can't grow in a healthy way if security is constantly shifting in a home, but loved ones can live without perfection. In fact, the more genuine security a wife or child feels, the more room they allow a person to fail. It's a bit like the farmer who goes to his banker and says, "I've got good news and bad news . . . ."

"Give me the bad news first," the banker says.

"Well, you know all that money I borrowed to buy that farm? I'm not doing well, so I don't have any money to pay you for it."

"Oh?" the banker says.

"Second, you know that money you loaned me for all that equipment, the tractor and everything? I can't pay for that either . . . ."

"No . . ." the banker moans.

"And third, all that money you loaned me for all the seeds? I can't pay that back either. I can't pay you anything."

"Well, what is the good news, for heaven's sake?" the banker wails.

"The good news is, I still want you to be my banker!"

My family knows I'm not perfect; they know I'll lose my temper at times—and they know I'm not always as sensitive as I should be. But one thing that helps them be patient with my imperfections is the knowledge that I'm 100 percent committed to them. I "still want them to be my banker," and I'm trying hard to be the kind of father and husband I should be. With each act of commitment, they see me with hammer and nail, adding on to a hallway of honor in our home.

For your wife or husband, a plaque in your hall may not spell security. But sometimes a loving symbol of our commitment acts like a wedding ring. The ring itself doesn't commit a person to marriage, but it shows to the world that the commitment has been made.

Perhaps for your spouse, security is a special event like a romantic dinner or going to a helpful marriage seminar like Campus Crusade's "Family Life Conference."[2] It may even be something as small as sending a card or calling home from the office each day just to see how your loved one is doing.

Norma has told me often that the way I "date" our kids makes her feel secure. I make it a practice to take my daughter Kari out on a special outing about once a month to show my commitment to Norma. The children are such an extension of her that simply knowing I am spending time with each child individually makes Norma feel secure in the strength and love I hold for our family.

Again, like a wise gardener, ask your spouse, "What is security to you?" Then take careful notes of what he or she says. Security may be spelled, "Let me have a say in the financial decisions," or "Take the time to have family devotions," or "Call me each day when you have to travel."

If you understand what "security" is to them, then you can begin making deposit after deposit into their love bank. This accrues high interest in your relationship. Just begin with a few simple questions like, "On a 1 to 10 scale, one being very '*insecure*' and ten being very '*secure,*' how confident do you feel in my love?" or "What could I specifically do over the next few months that would raise the level of security in our relationship?"

By seeking to build security into your spouse through small, positive acts, you do even more than add positive marks to the marital ledger. You also can help them (and yourself) to guard against the temptation to walk through a doorway named "dishonor."

The more security and honor we build into our homes—the tighter we help to shut the doorway to temptation for our loved ones. Interestingly, it's also the tighter we close the door to temptation for ourselves.[3]

The more "single minded" we are in our commitment to Christ, the less the distractions of the world pull upon us. The more "single minded" we are in building a "hall of honor" for our loved ones through honoring acts, the less room we leave for insecurity to dwell in our homes.[4]

There's a second way to develop security in a marriage that calls for the courage to make and keep an unconditional commitment to one's spouse. That commitment is often best seen in the sacrificial choices we may have to make if necessary.

2. Sacrificial Choices Are Also a Part of Providing Security

Betty waited in a little examination room in the doctor's office, her head lowered. Here it was, only two weeks before their only daughter's wedding, and she'd had another "lock-up" with her arthritis.

Once, Betty had been a cheerleader in the West Texas town in which she grew up. But you could never tell it now. Her heart and bubbly spirit were the same, but today (at fifty-five) they were trapped inside a body that was so crippled, she couldn't walk as well as most ninety-year-olds.

The constant pain from her joints flaring up had been bad, but the "lock-ups" were worst of all. Whenever she had a reaction to one of the "experimental" medicines prescribed for her, it was as if every joint in her body froze in place, and the pain and discomfort were almost unbearable.

Betty was a brave woman, but as she sat in the privacy of the doctor's office, tears rolled down her cheeks. She thought of her marriage to Rusty and all their dreams. She remembered all the plans they'd made for their retirement years . . . that would always remain as dreams. She thought of all the places they wanted to travel . . . but now never could. In her heart she knew that her arms were so battered by arthritis she'd never even be able to hold her first grandchild—the pain would simply be too great.

The door to the room opened, and her husband walked in from talking with the doctor. Looking over at his wife, he could see her chin trembling as she fought to regain her composure.

Try as she might, she couldn't help breaking into sobs.

"Oh, Rusty, please leave me," she begged him. "I'm getting worse, not better. I'm a mess. It hurts too much for you to touch me. I'm spending every cent we've saved toward retirement fighting this thing. I'm a burden to you and the kids and you know it."

Her tall, weather-beaten husband pulled over a chair and sat down beside her. Gently, he took her hand, twisted by arthritis, and said, "Sweetheart, it doesn't hurt to smile, does it? If you'll just smile at me now and then, that's all I need. I really don't even need that. I just need you."

Real love means a sacrificial, courageous commitment—especially when the other person may not be able to give back to you. None of our family members should have to feel what that little girl did when she saw her father's wedding ring bounce off the wall. Security should never be something you take on or off as you see fit. It's an abiding conviction that all is well with our commitment and all will be well—no matter what.

Sometimes sacrificial choices must be made in a marriage —but time and again they can heighten the security level in a home. Take Bill and Brenda for example.

Brenda had always wanted to be a veterinarian. However, she and Bill only had high school educations, and neither could really afford to go back to school. But Bill wouldn't let her dream die. He decided that she would go to school, regardless of the cost.

He knew what it meant to encourage her to get the training she'd need. He was looking at long hours spent on a second job in order for them to have the money for tuition. It took seven years of grueling work and sacrifice on both their parts for Brenda to become a vet, but the day finally came when she got her diploma. That meant her diplomas now outnumbered Bill's, three to one, but he couldn't have been happier—and neither could she. Their relationship didn't suffer because he had sacrificed his time and effort for his wife; it flourished.

Why does sacrifice add so much to a growing relationship? It should be obvious to those of us who live on this side of the Cross. That symbol of sacrifice is an unforgettable word picture of God's love for a lost world—and for each one of us who love Him.

Bill was simply following a biblical pattern when he built security into his marriage through sacrifice. After coming through the winter of a tough struggle together getting Brenda's degree, their marriage experienced an Alaskan summer where there's sunlight nearly twenty-four hours a day.

We've looked at building a "hallway of honoring actions" and making sacrificial choices to add sunlight and security to a marriage. There's a third way to raise the security level in a home, and that's to practice the kind of love that gets involved in another person's life in a very special way.

3. Building Security by Going Back to School

Recently, a close friend of ours, Jim Brawner, did a survey of several hundred teenagers at perhaps the top Christian sports camp in this country, Kamp Kanakuk in Branson, Missouri.[5] One of the first questions each boy or girl responded to on the questionnaire was: "*What is one tangible way your mother and/or father demonstrate that you're important to them?*" Can you guess what the number 1 response was, by far?

"I know they think I'm important because . . . they attended my games . . . my practices . . . my concerts . . . my open-houses . . . my band competitions . . . " In other words, with a teenager, security can be spelled with four words, "*Come and watch me!*"

While many men and women may not realize it, we never really outgrow the deep need we have for our loved ones to be excitedly supportive of our interests. What this means in a marriage is that the sunlight of security can shine on a marriage when we show an active interest in our loved one's life.

This was brought home to me in a tangible way when I first met a couple who became special friends. He was a huge offensive lineman for an NFL team when we first met, and his wife was perhaps 5'4" in heels. On the basis of size alone, there probably wasn't a more oddly matched pair. But in terms of their shared interests, this couple was only a heartbeat apart.

I met them at a Pro Athlete's Outreach Conference and was fascinated with a conversation we had at lunch one day. Out of curiosity, I asked this NFL wife how much she knew about the position her husband played on his team. I expected her to say something like, "Oh, he's paid to stand in front of other people." Instead, she gave me a ten-minute presentation on offensive blocking techniques.

Taken aback by her grasp of the sport, I asked how she'd become such an expert on her husband's position on the team. That's when she gave me a real-life lesson on what it does to become one's spouse's biggest fan—by becoming a graduate student of their likes and dislikes.

She explained that when they were first married, she resented the time he spent on the practice field, she resented all the team meetings and the travel. Finally, she grew tired of feeling so negative all the time, and she decided to go on the offensive. She would stop throwing spit-balls from the back row, and get up in the front row and learn about this career that she resented so much.

She began to ask her husband all sorts of questions about playing on the line for a pro team. She even cornered a few of the assistant coaches to learn more intricate details of the game. The more she learned and read, the more of an encourager she became. That's when a funny thing happened.

As her level of encouragement and interest went up, she noticed their marriage improving. While it wasn't her goal to get anything from her husband in return, he began showing more than a passing interest in her likes and dislikes.

What this wise woman had done was to push back the dark clouds of resentment to let the sunlight of security shine on her marriage. She didn't try to "coach" her husband, but her knowledge and interest in his life said clearly, "Because you're so important to me, your interests are important to me, too."

At the end of our conversation, my huge pro-football friend made a comment I've never forgotten: "Sometime I'll have to tell you how much my wife's taught me about refinishing antiques. I wouldn't be surprised if learning about one of her big interests is where I end up after football."

For this couple, being committed to each other meant showing interest in the things they individually valued. The message came over loud and clear that because of that attitude, they felt secure in each other's love and commitment. That security level showed clearly in their lives and the quality of love between them.

Like sunlight to a plant, the warmth of genuine security can be the first element a husband or wife gives to a successful relationship. In the next chapter, we'll look closely at a second crucial ingredient if intimacy is to grow. In fact, we'll introduce you to something we can do in our marriages that can act like life-giving water to our loved ones.

9

Meaningful Conversation: Life-giving Water to a Relationship

Most people take rain for granted—but not farmers. One of the most powerful black-and-white pictures I've ever seen is that of a dust-bowl farmer. He had waited over a year for rain, and now at last he had a chance. His face was turned up to the sky as the desperately needed rain poured down and mingled with his tears.

Every time I see this picture, it calls to mind what happens in many homes. In a marriage, meaningful words are like those raindrops. They can bring life-giving water to the soil of a person's life. In fact, all loving and meaningful relationships need the continual intake of the water of communication, or they simply dry up.

How many couples have I counseled who after fifteen or twenty years of marriage say, "What went wrong? Why is our marriage over?" Time after time, even casual conversation will show that instead of building a spring of consistent, meaningful conversation, they let the well run dry of encouraging words.

If that is the case—if meaningful, intimate conversation is like much needed water to a relationship—why is husband/wife communication often so difficult? Why do couples often learn what *not* to talk about, rather than what *to* talk about?

All too often encouraging words fall as infrequently as a dust bowl storm. Why? There are at least four natural roadblocks to meaningful communication that typically seem to emerge after the wedding day:

Roadblock # 1: Emotional Mind-Reading— or "Please Give Me a Clue!"

Because of a woman's natural sensitivity, nine times out of ten she will be the first one to spot a potential problem in a relationship. However, the problem can be so "obvious" to her that she can legitimately think, *Surely my husband is alert enough to see what the problem is. I'm not going to embarrass him by having to draw him a map.*

Yet, that's the very thing most men need! Give a man a road map of what issues are important to discuss, and often he'll be motivated to talk about them. But expect a husband to "sense" the subtleties (or even bold realities) of a marital or family concern, and often he won't see it as clearly.

Time and time again, I've been thankful for Norma's willingness to point out the "obvious" I've overlooked.

"Did you notice that Greg was acting a little down at the dinner table tonight?" she might ask.

"No, I didn't notice."

"Don't you think you ought to talk with him?" she'd persist.

"About what?" I'd ask. Like most men, I'm motivated to talk about facts. So far, Norma has been cluing me in on "feelings" and nonverbal behavior she's sensed that I've missed. I need "facts" to get really motivated about a conversation.

At this point, Norma could give up, throw up her hands and either go in and talk with Greg herself or chalk up another mark in the insensitivity column for me. But her love—and her knowledge of how to motivate me to communicate—doesn't let her stop here.

"Gary, I'm not sure if it's school, or the girl he's dating, or exactly what it is. But I can tell you that something is bothering Greg. Would you be willing to take your 'fact-finding' nature upstairs and *lovingly* find out how your son is doing?"

Rarely am I able to withstand Norma's call to go on the hunt for a problem to solve, and almost never has she been wrong in her sensitivity about one of the children.

The difference between mis-communication and meaningful communication often comes when a woman is willing to take the extra time to paint the obvious into a picture a man can clearly see or vice-versa. Mind-reading is never encouraged in the Scriptures, and while it may be part of an illusionist's act, it can wreak havoc in the realities of life at home.

Roadblock # 2:
"I No Speaka Your Language . . ."

In Chapter 4, you will recall we discussed the different "languages" that men and women often speak. In short, it seems that there is a "language of the heart" and a "language of the head" often spoken by women and men. Let me paint you a picture. Failing to tap into the unique conversational world of your spouse can cause this kind of frustration. It helps to illustrate a major mistake many women make in dealing with men. Namely, while trying to improve the level of meaningful communication in her home, a woman can inadvertently stifle the very thing she wants so much!

Let's say I walk into an auditorium where in a few short hours, Dr. Trent and I are going to give our "Love Is a Decision" seminar. I'm relaxed and looking forward to a great time with the couples and singles who'll be there, when all of a sudden I get one look at the room and nearly hyper-ventilate.

There's no doubt that this is the room and this is the night of the seminar—but there's also no denying that someone has made a major mistake! The chairs in the room are scattered all over, trash litters the floor, and the stage hasn't been set up. What's worse, with little time left before people begin coming early, I don't see anyone working to get things ready!

Frantically, I begin doing what I can to get the room in shape for the crowd that is bearing down on the auditorium. After ten minutes of going at a whirlwind pace, I notice a petite, bright-eyed woman sitting in a chair near the front row. Elated, I run over to her, and with a smile on my face and excitement in my voice I say, "Pardon me, but in a short time I'm going to be speaking at a conference in here, and I've got a real problem. If you don't have anything to do, could you give me a hand, please? Would you mind setting up some of these chairs while I pick up the trash and get the stage set up? Thank you so much for helping!"

She responds with a warm smile and nods her head, so I bound off like a big puppy, happy to have someone to help. The only problem is—two minutes later she's still sitting there. A little annoyed, I approach her again.

"Pardon me, Ma'am, but setting up chairs must not be your thing, so I'll tell you what. Could you help me with the stage, and I'll worry about the chairs and picking up the trash? Thank you so much for helping!" Once again she smiles and nods her head—but after another few minutes she's still sitting right in the same place.

Now I'm really irritated, and I come storming up to her and say,

"Pardon me, but . . . are you a Christian?"

I could get really angry at this woman and speak unkindly to her. That is until she opens her mouth and the words come out, "*Perdoneme, Senor. Yo no hablo Ingles. Puedo ayudarle a usted?*"

If I found out that this woman didn't speak a word of English, it would be pretty insensitive of me to stay angry at her, wouldn't it? But here's the very thing that many women do without even realizing it.

What many women fail to keep in mind is that their husbands genuinely may not see or understand the concerns that they're sharing. In many cases, they simply don't "speak-a" the language!

Getting angry and frustrated with a man to "motivate" him to a deeper level of understanding rarely works. Actually, it can make the surface soil of misunderstanding rock-hard and tougher than ever to penetrate.

Roadblock #3: Test the Soil of a Relationship to Determine Its Needed Moisture Level

As we've said, meaningful communication is like water to a growing relationship, but how do you find out how much "water" is needed in a marriage for maximum growth? Just as we found out that "security" needs are like sunlight to your spouse in the last chapter, in this chapter we'll look at what a nurturing husband or wife can do to encourage his or her partner. We'll find out how much meaningful communication he or she needs to feel fully watered. But let me make an observation.

I've asked hundreds of women in over sixty cities this question, "How much time do you need in meaningful conversation *each day* to feel really good about your relationship with your husband?" And time and again, the average woman answers that she needs at least *one hour a day* in intimate conversation to keep her marriage alive, thirst-free, and growing.

"An hour!" I can hear many men groaning. This can be a mammoth roadblock for many men. "Where am I going to find an hour a day?"

Before you panic, it's important to realize that the hour need not be spent in one block of time. Fifteen minutes in the morning as you trade places in front of the mirror getting ready for work, five minutes on the phone during the day, twenty minutes after work, fifteen minutes after the kids are down, five minutes before bed and then praying together can all be ways to bring needed moisture to your marriage.

We're not suggesting you put a stopwatch on your conversations (as one CPA friend did with the kitchen timer: "OK, Honey. We've got ten more minutes to talk. Now let's talk!") Exact time limits aren't important, but providing sufficient, consistent time to talk about important issues is.

To be accurate, I realize that an hour isn't necessarily the conversational need of every woman. One couple may be content with half an hour of talking, while another may need two hours to work through some difficult issues. Each couple must explore what best meets their needs, and consistently carve out the time from already overcrowded days to make sure their marriage stays a priority. The important thing to realize is that if communication is like life-giving water, a marriage will yellow and brown out if this necessary ingredient for growth is insufficient.

Why Try to Take the Road At All If There Are So Many Roadblocks?

At this point you may be saying, "What's the use? We're so hopelessly different, we'll never be able to understand each other or be able to reach any kind of intimacy."

That's not true. Time and time again, we've seen the natural "incompatibility" of the two sexes become the very grounds for a great marriage. Rather than retreating into frustration, silence, or verbal explosions, why not take the time to master two specific communication skills that can re-vitalize your communication. These two particular skills help take conversations to a level many never dreamed possible.

The first of these skills is to employ the most powerful communication tool we know of in the Scriptures. We call these emotional word pictures, and without exaggeration, we've seen it turn forty-watt communication into a laser beam of words that hits both head and heart at the same time.

One Emotional Word Picture Is Worth a Thousand Words

"An emotional word picture is a communication tool that simultaneously activates a person's emotions and intellect. In so doing, it causes another person to not just hear our words, but experience them."[2]

Some of the greatest communicators in history have used word pictures to inspire patriotism, lead nations, and direct the course of history. George Washington and Thomas Jefferson did so in our early history. Abraham Lincoln credited Harriet Beecher Stowe with the North's involvement in the Civil War, claiming that once it got a picture of what slavery was like, there was no turning back. The picture she used? *Uncle Tom's Cabin.*[3] Roosevelt and John F. Kennedy, even Ronald Reagan in more recent times, all salted their political and public speeches with word pictures. For all the good these have done, tragically, many evil leaders like Hitler and Jim Jones have also been masters at using this powerful form of communication.

Without question, the greatest use of word pictures is seen in the Scriptures. Throughout the pages of the Old and New Testament, we are taught the greatest lessons of faith the Bible has to offer through word pictures.

What could be more descriptive of what our attitude should be toward God than King David's picture, "As the deer pants for streams of water, so my soul pants for you, O God" (Psalm 42:1)? Or what could more graphically describe God's love for a stubborn, hard-hearted people than Hosea's relationship with the prostitute Gomer and how it represented God's love for the lost?

What's a clearer picture of the call to a life of faith than of an athlete, training diligently and running hard so as to win the prize (Philippians 3:14)? And, what Christian serious about caring for a lost world has ever casually glanced at the portrait of the Good Samaritan and not been convicted to reach out (Luke 10)?

There's no doubt that word pictures are a powerful way to communicate. They take our words right to another person's heart and also lock them inside their memory. For now, let's look at a few examples of word pictures illustrated in relationships. See if they don't grab your attention more than everyday words.

Let's say a woman usually finds herself saying to her husband: "I'm sick of being ignored around here. You're always watching television." To which he could reply: "Now, honey, am I *always* watching television. Did I watch TV *this morning*? Did I watch it anytime during the day *yesterday*?" (Remember, if you share feelings with a man—the language of the heart)—you're likely to get an answer back in facts—(the language of the head.)

Instead of the same overworked phrases that really don't address the real concern (which is not he is "always" watching television but her feelings of being ignored), you could use a word picture to carry your words.

The wife could ask: "Honey, can we talk sometime soon, right now or tonight if it's better, about something that's been concerning me?" When they do sit down to talk in a quiet setting, the wife could *hand her husband the remote control unit* from the television set. Instead of the standard lecture, she could say:

"Do you know how I'm feeling right now? When you watch TV, you use the remote control device to skip past something you don't like and turn to something really interesting. For the past several weeks, I've been feeling like I'm one of the channels on your set—one of the ones you skip past when you're looking for something really interesting to watch.

"In fact, when my face finally does come up on the screen, you either click the remote to the next channel or put it on 'mute.' On the few times you do leave me on the screen, I feel as if I'm talking and talking to you, but you're just staring at me as if you can't hear a word I'm saying.

"What I want to know is what it would take to have you get your finger off the mute button so I could get some 'air time' to talk about some issues that I feel are very important."

Or instead of a man saying to his wife over and over: "That's it. I've had it with you nagging me. I'll tell you when I'm going to fix the fence. *When I'm good and ready, that's when*! That is unless you keep bugging me—in which case I'll put it off even longer!"

He could use a word picture to communicate his frustration:

"Sweetheart, we've got to talk. Can I ask you a question? How would you feel if you were with the two little ones at the grocery store, and every cash register had a huge line behind it? And not only that, after you finally picked a line, the check-out lady decides to go on a break when you're two people from the front. That means you have to go all the way to the end of another long line and wait all over again, and all the time you're waiting in line, the kids are acting up and arguing with each other and embarrassing you. How would that make you feel?"

Certainly, if she'd experienced such a day at the store she'd be very frustrated, and after hearing her response, he could say:

"Well, you may not realize it, but that's exactly what's going on at work lately. With the move coming up and my having to work with so many different departments and problems, I feel as if I've had to stand in one line to order new equipment, then get in another line to get the space in the new building to put it in. Then I find out that I can't have the space, and I'm back in line, having to start all over again. All the time there are people running around pestering me with little problems and making things really frustrating.

"Finally, after standing in lines all day, I come home from work, and you tell me there's another chore you want me to do. I know that the house and the fence are important to you, but right now, I feel as if I'm standing in so many lines at work, I just can't get in the 'fence' line until we finish our move in three weeks. Can I have a 'time out' from reminders to fix the fence until the move is done at work?"

Do Word Pictures Really Motivate a Person to Change His Behavior?

Word pictures can help make the hard work of a relationship easier by providing the initial motivating factor in getting the process of change started. My own family continually uses word pictures with me because they're so powerful. Recently my daughter Kari shared a word picture with me that motivated me to change an out-of-balance attitude I had with my youngest son, Michael.

We were driving home from a vacation in our rented motor home. We had been gone for about five days, and it was about ten o'clock at night as we finally headed back to Phoenix. Everyone else was asleep when twenty-two-year-old Kari came up to sit by me. It brought back special memories of old times, as it seemed that she was always the one who would "stay up and talk to Daddy to help keep him awake" when she was a little girl. Only this time, instead of talking about her dreams or dating, she said: "Dad, there's something I want to talk to you about. . . . But it can wait until we get back home."

"No, go ahead," I said. "We've got nothing but time."

"But I don't know exactly how to explain this to you," she said.

"Why don't you try to think up a word picture?" I suggested.

"Okay," she said. I jogged her thoughts by saying, "Pick some area that's very familiar to me." We drove on in silence for a few moments as she thought up a word picture.

"Okay, I've got one," she finally announced.

"Pretend that you're giving a seminar somewhere, and it's a really big one. I mean like 2,000 people in the conference. On the first night, you're really funny and warm, and everybody's responded well. They all can't wait for the next day.

"But the next morning when the seminar starts, you're not warm or funny at all. In fact, you spend the whole time criticizing them—even when a lot of them really don't deserve it. You say things like, 'I'm fed up with all of you. You go to church and read the Bible but you don't really love your family like you should!' Or you say, 'I'm so sick of the way some of you wives hound your husbands, it's push, push, push all the time!!! And you men, why don't you grow up and be the lovers you're supposed to be?'

"What would happen to the people in the audience, Dad, if you spent the entire morning criticizing them?"

I said, "Kari, I probably wouldn't have an audience very long. Undoubtedly some of the people would get up and leave as soon as I got started—and many more would begin leaving at the first break. They'd say, 'Why am I sitting here listening to this junk? Who does he think he is? He doesn't even know my situation. . . .'"

I thought for a moment—not realizing that I was digging myself a deeper grave—and said, "You know in Proverbs it says, 'Pleasant words are a honeycomb, sweet to the soul and healing to the bones.' I pray that God will help me speak that way. I don't want to come across harsh."

Kari said, "Dad, I hate to say this to you, but this is probably more true of you than you realize. You see, Michael lives at one of those seminars every day where you are criticizing people —only he's a captive audience. He can't get up and leave like those people when you criticize him."

I couldn't have been stopped any shorter if I had just hit a brick wall with the camper. Perhaps it's because Michael is so much like me, but I have had to battle a tendency to "pick, pick, pick" on little things he does. "Mike, chew with your mouth closed. Mike, don't drink out of that. Mike, don't. . . ." At the time of this writing, it's been a year since Kari hit me with that word picture, and I have yet to forget it.

Kari's word picture literally changed my behavior on the spot, because her words turned into a laser beam and hit me right in the heart. The first thing I did when Michael woke up that morning was to ask his forgiveness. For a year now Kari's word picture has been my constant reminder that I'm to be his greatest encourager—not his strongest critic. Word pictures can be extremely effective, but just as with any skill, we have to learn the basics—and practice them.

Becoming an Expert One Step at a Time

When I first learned to ski, the instructor had to show us how to do it one step at a time. That was frustrating at first, because I saw all these expert skiers gracefully gliding down the slopes, and all the time I was feeling like a pigeon-toed duck with two left feet. He kept drilling us on different skills involved, and after a while I became so dejected that I never thought I'd be able to ski like everyone else, but I was wrong.

Deep-seated problems don't vanish instantly without consistent work by the couple and relying on God's strength for daily endurance.

Bit by bit, as I practiced what he taught, I began to wed one skill to another. Pretty soon, I could get out on the slopes and not have to think, *Plant your pole, pressure on the downhill ski, lean into the turn, turn around the pole, slide the uphill ski alongside.* After practicing time and again, it just came naturally! Now I enjoy skiing more than I ever thought I could.

It's the same way with word pictures. At first, you may feel awkward and discouraged when you try to use them. Each step may seem tedious. But keep at it! You'll get the hang of it quicker than you think. Soon you'll be a master at using them.[4]

Time and again we've seen frustrated, tense relationships transformed as committed couples have used word pictures. This change in their lives doesn't happen by magic. Deep-seated problems don't vanish instantly without consistent work from the couple and a reliance on God's strength for daily endurance. But word pictures can and do bring change—particularly as people discover this powerful pattern of "picture talk" set down in the Scriptures.

If word pictures are the most powerful method of communicating we know, there is a second aspect to communicating that any healthy home shouldn't be without. This method has saved many a conversation from deteriorating into a distasteful argument. It works by slowing down what we say—in order to quick listen!

The Effectiveness of Slowing Down to Quick Listen!

During my morning run one day, I thought of something I could do as a loving act for Norma. I decided that since we were going camping that afternoon, I'd volunteer to pack the camper. She could go to breakfast with her good friend Helen and have a great time while I got our things stowed away.

I increased my pace, and when I got home, I said, "Hey, do I have a surprise for you!"

"What's that?" Norma asked.

"What do you think about calling Helen and the two of you going out to breakfast this morning? I'll do all the packing for the trip."

"Hmmmph," she said as she turned and walked away. It was not exactly the reaction I was anticipating.

"What's wrong?" I said, following her. That's when she said something that I couldn't believe I was hearing:

"You've been thinking for a long time how you could take over the packing, haven't you?"

I was stunned. "No!" I answered emphatically.

She responded by saying, "Then why do I get the feeling you think you can pack the camper better than I'm doing it?"

"WHAT?" At that moment, I wanted to tell her *she* could go ahead and pack the camper and *I'd* go to breakfast with Helen.

When the initial anger subsided, I realized she thought I was coming from a totally different direction, but before we got into a major blowout, I decided we needed to do a little *quick listening* to straighten things out.

"Why are you reacting to me like this?" I asked.

"Because I know that secretly you don't like the way I pack the camper."

"You mean you think I made up the thing about you going to breakfast with Helen so I could get you out of the way and pack the camper. Is that right?"

"Yes, exactly."

"Norma! That wasn't it at all. I was trying to think of something loving I could do for you today."

She paused, "You're saying that you were trying to do something *nice* for me?"

"As strange as it may seem, *Yes!*"

By doing some quick listening, I was able to clarify exactly what she thought the issue was, allow her the opportunity to see that I truly understood her, and then correct the misperception in our communication. By listening rather than reacting, I was able to avoid a major confrontation.

Quick listening is simply one technique you can use to help you understand what the other person is really saying. It slows conversation to a pace that both of you can manage. Surprisingly, in our high-speed world, putting thoughts in low gear can move understanding ahead more quickly.

It's a helpful tool to use when an argument is about to erupt, and it is also very useful in everyday conversation to clarify meaning and enhance understanding. It helps you talk through problems succinctly and more clearly, and forces you to make your statements fairly. There are just three simple steps in mastering the art of quick listening.

Three Steps to "Quick" Listening

1. Try to Recognize the Issue behind the Issue

Let's say you and I are having a discussion and are having difficulty understanding one another. Using quick listening, I can honor you by giving you the opportunity to clarify what you're saying first. It lets you know that I'm genuinely concerned and interested in what you're saying—and that I'm making an effort to understand you. It relaxes you because you realize I'm more interested in comprehending what you say than conquering the discussion. It also allows me another opportunity to hear what you're trying to say.

With Norma, the issue wasn't breakfast with Helen. The issue that was at the heart of her hurt feelings was her sensitivity in thinking I was really criticizing the way she packed the camper. We could have talked all day about my words, but when we slowed the conversation down to talk about the issue *behind* the words and her reaction, we quickly came to an understanding of the real problem.

2. Restate What the Other Person Has Said in Your Own Words

After the other person has had the opportunity to summarize what they've said, I can respond, "Now let me repeat what you've said to make sure I understand." I can then verbalize what they've said to see if I've actually received the message *they* meant to communicate.

If I have it right, they'll say, "Yes, that's it." If not, they can say, "No." Then I can restate what they've said. Again, that's what I did with Norma. I had to slow things down and ask her specifically—by repeating her words—if she felt that I was criticizing her instead of helping her. It's my responsibility at that point to keep asking questions and rewording her statement until I get a "yes." When I do, it's my turn to tell her how I feel. That way we're both honored in what is said.

3. Lovingly Confine What You Say

Using too many words during an important discussion can actually break down intimate conversation. When we talk in long, rambling paragraphs instead of short concise statements, we increase the chances the listener has for reacting to what we say, without really understanding it. If we continue to add words without clarifying the issues and feelings we have, the other person can become so frustrated or bored that he'll tune us out altogether.

Learning to be brief isn't always as easy as it sounds. Not too long ago, I took an intensive two-day course in Los Angeles on how to be interviewed on television, radio, and for a newspaper. The first day I felt like a dismal failure. The instructors kept trying to get me to be brief and to the point, and I just couldn't do it.

"Now, Gary," one said, "you have to summarize the most important part of your message in one sentence." After years of being "wordy" by nature, I couldn't do it. She kept stopping the tape and making me try again and again.

"Gary, you said that in five sentences. I said *one!*" my coach would insist. "If you're going to get your message across on television, you've got to be brief. People may like to read about details, but on television or in person they won't stay with you for five sentences."

By the second day, I was doing much better. When I concentrated on what I was saying, I was amazed that I could use half as many words and say twice as much. I love to talk, so, take heart—if *I* can slow down and summarize my conversations, *anyone* can!

Often, couples need to limit their words to increase their understanding of each other. Once, while counseling a couple where the wife rarely stopped talking to listen, I had to break in on her: "I'm sorry, but if you really want your husband to spend time with you, I have to be honest." We were close enough friends for me to say, "You've got to make a decision to confine yourself to saying things with a fewer number of words. I'm getting bored listening to you, and I'm the counselor! Remember that confining your words and listening to what he has to say is one of the most loving acts you can do."

God has endowed some of us with a love for the spoken word. That's tremendous, but sometimes we can get carried away! As did the wife mentioned above, we can lose our audience of one as a result.

Quick listening has stopped numerous arguments from flaring around the Smalley household, and I know it can make a difference in your family as well. We've made a conscious decision not to let our anger stay around longer than the sun going down and to make every effort to honor one another through greater understanding.

Proverbs 14:29 says, "He who is slow to anger has great understanding, but he who is quick tempered exalts folly." One of the keys to any healthy relationship is a willingness to say, "I'm more interested in understanding what you're saying to me than in thinking of what I'm going to say once you're done talking." Quick listening is one of the best ways I know to help others discover what you're thinking—and what they're thinking as well.

In the previous chapter, we looked at how a husband or wife needs to provide security as bright sunlight in which a relationship can grow. Now we've seen that meaningful communication is like a summer rain shower to encourage such growth. These are two of the four essential elements a loving "nurturer" needs to grow a strong marriage or family.

Now let's go on to discover a third important element of a loving home. It is every bit as important as soil is to a healthy root system. At the same time, we'll be uncovering a secret to keep courtship alive in marriage for years on end.

10

Keeping Courtship Alive in Marriage

Without a doubt, this was going to be the most romantic evening of their entire marriage. Of course, they'd only been married a year, but Greg knew his surprise for Sharon would redefine the word "romance."

Unbeknownst to his wife, Greg had taken off work early to get ready for their anniversary. He knew his wife's favorite thing was to enjoy dinner at a place with a beautiful view, so he came up with the ultimate restaurant—*on top of a nearby mountain*!

Greg spent five hours carrying a table, chairs, a Coleman stove, ice, and drinks up to the pinnacle of a small peak near their home. In his mind's eye, he saw the two of them sharing a wonderful dinner together, complete with thousands of city lights sparkling below them like candles. And after a romantic dinner . . . *who knows*?

All that remained for him to do was to drive to his wife's work-place, surprise her, and make the climb to the intimate nest he'd created on top of the world. Greg had thought of everything . . . except his wife's interests and response. For from the moment he "surprised" her at work, his beautiful plan began to unravel.

First, she was so tired from a grueling day of fighting office politics that she wanted to stay home and rest—not go out for a long evening. Then when he pulled out her climbing boots, she said she was too tired to climb anything—and she wasn't really hungry anyway.

Greg didn't want to give away his carefully arranged surprise. (Besides, he knew they had an hour up-hill ahead of them just to reach the summit.) So he demanded that she "quit griping" and start climbing.

Reluctantly, she trudged up the mountain to where the wind

had kicked up and blown over most of his campsite. Then the campstove wouldn't light . . . and the ice had melted . . . and the wind kept blowing dirt all over the table . . . and he'd forgotten the forks.

Finally, dinner was served but Sharon was so tired from climbing and nearly being blown off the mountain-top, she said she'd pass on eating. In total frustration, Greg ripped off the tablecloth, sending dishes flying everywhere. This only caused her to begin to cry and him to begin to fume.

Instead of walking down the mountain arm in arm in the moonlight that night, they stumbled down the now pitch-dark trail in silence (naturally, he'd forgotten a flashlight). The ice for their drinks may have melted up on the mountain-top—but the wall of ice between them was as thick as a brick wall as they drove home!

Greg had the right idea. He was trying to add an important element to their marriage that is missing for many couples. Unfortunately, he missed some important aspects of this third important way to nurture a marriage.

Keeping Courtship Alive in Your Marriage

During courtship, romance is something that seems to overflow naturally. Let the years of marriage pass, however, and often romance slows to a thin trickle. Yet romance is an essential ingredient of a strong relationship. Most women admit it is lacking in their home, and most men confess inability and failure in supplying it.

Actually, romance is not unique to our day. It has filled stories since the beginning of time, but with our Hollywood images of intimacy, for many of us it's difficult ever to experience the real thing. While it may not seem as important as meaningful communication or keeping a person's spirit open, romance is still an essential element to building the kind of loving, lasting relationships we've been discussing.

Romance finds its place in a marriage right between the chapters that illustrate love as a decision of our will, and the sexual relationship which involves our feelings and emotions. In many ways, romance is the bridge between the two. It's an important way we express honor to our spouse, and it provides the basis for a meaningful sex life.

Poetically, we could say that romance is the flame which glows on the candle of unconditional love; it's the act of honor that soothes and refreshes a marriage like a gentle spring rain; it's the fertile soil in which passion grows. But for those of us who didn't major in poetry, what is it in plain English?

Romance is the act of keeping your courtship alive long after the wedding day. Put another way, romance is an intimate friendship, celebrated with expressions of love reserved only for each other.

***R**omance is the act of keeping your courtship alive long after the wedding day.*

Ground Rules for Helping Romance Blossom

In some ways, romance breaks open the deepest feelings of a person. Greg had hoped that all his special efforts would show Sharon how excited he was that she was his wife. He had sought to create a natural setting that would open up her life to a deeper intimacy. Instead, his relationship took a fall from the mountaintop. Why? For the same reason that many couples struggle in keeping courtship alive in their marriage. They need to follow several practical ground-rules to keep romance on the right trail to intimacy.

The most common reason why romance dies in a relationship is that it gets inseparably linked to physical intimacy. Often this happens because that's the way television or movies paint the scene. It's as if any display of tenderness or emotional intimacy is simply a warm-up for the main act of physical intimacy, but while effective romance may *sometimes* lead to sex, our goal in being romantic shouldn't be sex.

God certainly created men to be goal-oriented initiators. He filled their bodies with a wonderful chemical that heightens their sex drive (see Chapter 11). Sometimes, though, we allow our natural enthusiasm to get the best of us and make the fundamental mistake of substituting emotional closeness with a physical experience.

If the only time I take my wife's hand is to say, "Let's go to bed," I'm ignoring her need for romantic times apart from the bedroom. For most women, it's almost as if God has wonderfully crafted them with a built-in "relational safety switch" that won't allow a few moments of pleasure to be a counterfeit for a meaningful relationship.

If romance is more than just making sure the hallway's clear to the bedroom, what is it? First, it's

Friendship, Not Foreplay

In his book, *Romancing Your Marriage,* Norm Wright quotes a couple who define romance this way:

> Romance is not a setting. . . . It's a *relationship* which can be taken into and out of a wide variety of settings.[1]

I like that! Romance is a *relationship,* not an event. It's not something we do occasionally to stoke the fires of passion. Rather, it should be an ongoing, foundational part of our relationship, something that doesn't come and go like the tide, but flows as steadily as a river. An inescapable aspect of romance is being "best friends" with your spouse.

In the Song of Solomon, Solomon praises his bride saying, "This is my lover, this my friend . . ." (5:16). During the ideal courtship, couples should have time to build their friendship to its peak. Why is friendship so closely linked to romance?

Can you think back to "your song" on the radio, your table at a favorite restaurant, your secret way of holding hands? During courtship, an entire nation may be listening to the same love song on the radio—but that same song creates a special bond between the two of you.

A key to blending friendship with romance is to take the

time to explore each other's interests and then share them together. I recently saw a cartoon that captures this idea. The scene shows a couple walking happily hand in hand, looking deeply into each other's eyes, and obviously enjoying a conversation together. The caption reads, "Romance happens when . . . he asks about her potted plants and she asks about the football scores." As unromantic as "sunflowers" and "screen passes" may seem, that cartoon really captures the essence of one important element of romance.

If you're not growing a friendship based on each other's shared interests—I can almost guarantee you that the romantic soil in your relationship is lacking the essential nutrients it needs. I learned this the hard way one summer when a "romantic" getaway did nothing but push Norma away from me.

Missing the Forest for the Trees

For years one of the things that I thought would be a "10" romantically would be to take a long camping trip to the Colorado mountains with Norma. This would be a special, two-week trip where we took scenic back roads to the most beautiful places in the state, visited historic spots, and stayed in campgrounds or even out in the wild. After years of prodding, I finally convinced my wife it would be a great experience, so we loaded up and headed for the hills.

Less than half-way through the trip, Norma was beside herself. She finally broke down and said, "I don't know how much longer I can take this. There are no malls around, no cute shops, and no restaurants. I can't handle another day of this, much less another week. Can't we camp in the mountains close to a town so we could walk to it and see some other people or shop for the kids?"

At first I was angry that she was trying to ruin my "romantic" dream vacation. I even drove nonstop from Colorado to Flagstaff, Arizona, without saying one word to her on the way home. Later, I apologized for my actions, and I realized I had never thought of asking what would be a romantic trip for *her.* I wasn't interested in what she was interested in; I had my own romantic adventure in mind, even though it was hopelessly boring for her.

Fortunately, even if we feel helpless in picking a romantic

experience, there's something a man or a woman can specifically do to help turn one's spouse into the hopeless romantic we'd like him or her to be.

What's Your Ten?

Contrary to popular opinion, close romantic times don't just happen. With our over-committed lifestyles, if we don't set our schedules, someone or something else will set them for us. Since the chances to make great memories together come and go so quickly, it's important to take advantage of opportunities for romance that come our way.

Planning is the key. I know, some of you are thinking, *But Gary! . . . Planning takes all the thrill out of it. Romance is supposed to be spontaneous*! No doubt spontaneity has its place; we'll look at that in a moment. For now, though, it's crucial we rid ourselves of the false notion that the secret to building a romantic relationship is the five o'clock phone call for a candlelight dinner at six.

By planning, what I mean is using the "twenty questions" method with your spouse. This is something we've done at seminars across the country, and it's amazing the amount of "romantic" information you can get in a short time. If you remember, Chapter 4 listed questions a husband can ask a wife that can revolutionize their relationship. Each question uses the "one to ten" scale to gauge the other's response.

The same is true here. Husbands and wives should begin blending their recipe for romance together with:

"Honey, on a scale of one to ten, what's a romantic ten to you?"

It's a good idea to have paper and pen ready, to jot down each idea that is suggested. Next, "milk" these answers for added information. By "milking" I mean try to find out as much information as possible about what your spouse has told you by asking more questions about the idea.

For instance, if your spouse says, "I think it would be a ten to go on a skiing vacation," then you could ask, "Where would you want to go? What time of the year? What kind of snow would you like best? Would you need new ski clothes? What colors and styles? Where would we eat? Where would you like to stay?

Would we meet friends there or go by ourselves? Would we do anything else besides ski?" The list could go on and on.

Each question you ask makes you a more insightful romantic. The more you know about what would be a "ten" for your spouse, the more you'll be able to understand his or her interests, and become more fully involved in them.

Not too many of us are able to schedule a week's skiing as a vacation, which leads to a very important principle we need to keep in mind. *The success of romantic times together has very little to do with how much money we spend.* If successful, romantic relationships depended on the size of our bank account, most of us wouldn't even have a nodding acquaintance! Focusing on money as the secret to sharing one another's interests will rob us of some of the most romantic times we'll ever spend.

Steve Lyon, one of our invaluable staff members, recently had no money in his pocket and an open Sunday afternoon. Sensing his wife's, Brenda's, need to get out of the house, he loaded her and their baby girl into the car and drove to a downtown civic and arts center.

Sidewalk vendors were selling trendy T-shirts, jewelry, and ice cream; couples and families sat on a plush carpet of green grass listening to a brass quartet. Fountains flowed with the gentle sounds of bubbling water, and the art museum was open free of charge. They didn't buy *anything*—not even an ice cream bar or a glass of lemonade.

Two hours later, they were relationally richer and not a penny poorer. Brenda would later say, "That was one of the most romantic times we've had in months." Surprising, isn't it? Not to a man who knew his wife's love and interest in art and who took time that could have gone into a Sunday nap to create a romantic memory in her life.

So who cares if you can't jet to the Rockies and schoosh down a mountain? Spend a Saturday morning hunting down garage sales or going for a frozen yogurt. Your romance will never be better, even if your wallet isn't bulging with money! (Later, we'll share twenty-five low-cost ideas on keeping courtship alive.)

Why not sit down with your spouse and look at the year ahead? Find out each other's romantic tens, and schedule what you can into the calendar. It's amazing what anticipation does to heighten romance! Be sure to commit to making these dates a priority. If you don't, other things or other people will crowd them out of your schedule.

At our house, we sometimes know what we'll be doing a year in advance. Most families don't plan that far ahead, but my work requires me to plan so that other things don't choke the romance out of our relationship. Norma and I talk about special times we'll have together as a family (something I discuss more fully in Chapter 12), but we make sure we reserve some special time just for the two of us.

Developing a deep level of friendship through shared interests is the first essential ingredient in a romantic relationship. Discovering each other's relational "tens" and making plans to make them happen can also make a huge difference in the quality of our romantic times together. There's a third way of keeping the courtship alive with our spouse. It's found in learning to . . .

Celebrate the Moments of Your Life

Those who are wise romantics will realize that some special date or event every year can be used to fan the romantic flame. I recall one man who did put together a very special celebration for his wife to honor her for a sacrifice she had made for him.

It was the eve of his graduation from a long, grueling master's degree program. Four years of intensive, full-time study had finally found him about to receive his diploma.

His wife planned a special party where many of their friends were to come and help him celebrate the long awaited "day of deliverance." There would be cake, refreshments, banners, streamers, a pool nearby, croquet, and other yard games. Many people had already accepted her invitation to come, and it looked like it would be a full house. Her husband, though, had other ideas. He secretly contacted each person who had received an invitation and told them he wanted to make the party a surprise in honor of *her*. Yes, there would be banners, streamers, and all the rest, but they would bear her name, not his.

He wanted to do something special to let her know how much he appreciated the years of sacrifice she'd devoted to his graduation. Working full time to put him through, and putting off her dreams of a house and family, had, in many ways, been harder on her than the long hours of study had been on him.

When the day arrived, she was busy with preparations and last minute details, still convinced that all was going according to plan. He arranged to get her away from the party site, and while she was gone, he put up a huge banner with her name on it. During that time all the guests arrived as well.

She returned to be greeted with a huge "SURPRISE!!!" and when she realized what was going on, she could barely fight back the tears. Her husband asked a few people to share what they most appreciated about her. Then he stood before them and, with tender words of love and appreciation, expressed his gratitude for all she'd done for him. When he was through, they saluted her with an iced-tea toast.

The rest of the evening was a fun-filled fiesta of laughing, catching up with one another, water volleyball, yard games, and more food than anyone could eat. It was a celebration of an experience they both shared, and by commemorating it in a special way, this husband created a lifelong, romantic memorial to his wife's love and dedication.

Birthdays, anniversaries, or holidays can become more than simply a traditional observance. They can be a personal opportunity to let your loved one know they are very special to you—in ways they'll never forget.

Creative Romance: Surprise, Surprise, Surprise!

We've seen that building a friendship around shared interests and tapping into times of special celebration, can strengthen the romantic bonds in a relationship. There's another aspect of romance that, if not overused, can also be a real help in a home, for if it's true that the element of surprise has won countless battles, it's equally true that it has won the hearts of untold lovers.

A young man in our home church recently pulled off a romantic surprise that's one of the best I've ever heard. It's something his wife-to-be will never forget, and it will make a great story for his grandchildren one day.

It was a beautiful, clear desert morning. The sun was still minutes away from its grand entrance, but it teased the Eastern sky with a hundred shades of gold. The mountains kept their silent sentinel in the cold, crisp dawn, the brilliant stars shining behind them like silver sequins on black velvet.

"WHHHOOOOOOOSSSHH," the sound of the hot-air balloon's burner broke the desert's quiet with resounding force. In a few heartbeats, its brilliant blue and red canopy sprang to life and lifted off the ground. It floated upward, carrying a basket with Steve, Jan, and the pilot cradled inside.

Going up in a hot-air balloon was something they'd both wanted to do for a long time, and now they were in the air! In just a few moments, they were several hundred feet up, gliding along with the wind's gentle currents.

The scene was spectacular, and while Steve and Jan were busy enjoying the moment, the pilot was making sure the flight continued to go smoothly.

All at once, the incredible quiet was broken by the distinct drone of an engine. At first, Jan thought it must be the sound of a truck on the road below them, but then she realized it was getting louder. Startled, Jan looked up to see an airplane headed right for them! She was paralyzed with fear—but if she had looked at Steve or the pilot, she'd have seen them both smiling.

The plane Steve had hired to "buzz" the hot air balloon was right on time. When it turned close to them, a long tail appeared behind it revealing a message that read, in larger-than-life letters, "*I love you, Jan. Will you marry me?*"

When the words on the banner finally hit her, she was beside herself; she jumped up and down in the confines of the balloon basket like a six-year-old on Christmas morning. "Yes, I'll marry you!" she said, laughing and crying at the same time. For this couple, a special surprise was an indication that creative romance would stay a part of their relationship.

Surprising ways to say "I love you" aren't reserved for restricted air-space. They can be a note put in a lunch-box, a cassette tape with a loving greeting put in the car's tape player in secret, a frozen yogurt that arrives with you at your husband's office on a hot, summer's afternoon. Planning can make sure that romance stays a consistent part of your relationship. But surprises can make the moment a cherished one. These actions all say, *I'm thinking about you, my love for you is secure, you're important to me, we're together for life.*

But I'm Just Not Creative. . . .

I once had a friend who worked with high school students in Young Life. He was one of the funniest, most creative people I'd ever met. One day I asked him his "secret" for being creative, and he told me, "My definition of creativity is forgetting who I borrowed the idea from."

Now, that might not work in writing books, but it certainly points out that even if you're unfortunate enough to have come up with a "zero" in the ingenuity department—there's still hope. Just draw together ideas from the hopeless romantics around, forget where you borrowed them, and put them into practice!

It's not so much coming up with good ideas on your own, it's knowing where to find them and then knowing how to make them work. It's important to have a good resource for creative, romantic ideas. Let me suggest two:

Tapping into Creative Ideas for Romantic Times

The first source is your spouse. Sometimes we overlook this tremendous resource because it's so obvious. If you ask your spouse, "Honey, what's a romantic ten to you?" you can potentially receive a wealth of ideas. Most people have a list of things that will strike them as creatively romantic.

One of the cornerstones of creativity is this: *Ideas give birth to more ideas.* Something your spouse says may trigger an idea in your mind for a creative way to pull it off. Be alert to this possibility as you talk together. Whatever you do, be sure to *write down your ideas.* Try to keep your "Recipes for Romance" notebook within reach as much as possible.

The second is collecting lists of romantic ideas. These can be found in a variety of places, but several of them are right in your local Christian bookstore. *Four Hundred Creative Ways to Say I Love You* by Alice Chapin is a great resource.[2] So is a chapter entitled "Keeping Romance Alive," in *Romancing Your Marriage* by Norm Wright.[3] *Men, Do You Know Your Wife?* by Dan Carlinsky[4] is a helpful way to get to know things about your wife that will no doubt spark some creativity.

Let me add a few ideas of my own . . .

Twenty Creative, Romantic Ideas That Cost under $20

1. Dress up for a meal you bring back from your favorite fast food restaurant. Take out a tablecloth, centerpiece, and a tape

recorder of your favorite romantic music and dine to a "Golden Arches" delight.

2. Buy a half gallon of your favorite ice cream, go to the most beautiful park in town, throw a blanket on the ground, and eat the whole thing.

3. Visit a museum or art gallery. Talk with each other about the art you like and dislike. Use the "twenty questions" method to learn all you can about why your spouse likes or dislikes what you see. Concentrate on listening to the other person and learning all you can from what he or she says.

4. Go to a driving range together. Cheer each other's good shots.

5. Go bowling together. Come up with prizes you can give each other for winning games; i.e., a massage, a week's worth of doing dishes, a promise to paint the fence, etc.

6. Go on a hay-ride with four other couples, singing camp songs from a tape recorder or guitar. Plan a cookout under the stars afterward.

7. Write love notes to one another and hide them in unusual places like the freezer, a shoe, in the car's glove box, in the bathtub, in a makeup kit, or under the bed covers.

8. Go snorkeling in a lake.

9. Collect leaves and pine cones together on an autumn day. Take them home and make fall ornaments for the house.

10. Attend a free outdoor concert.

11. Buy a pass from the Forest Service, go to a National Forest, and cut your own Christmas tree.

12. Buy a modern paraphrase of the Song of Solomon and read it to one another.

13. Walk hand in hand along a nature trail.

14. Watch a sunset together.

15. Make "dough" ornaments together, bake them, and then color them with the kids.

16. Rent each other's all-time favorite movies and play a double feature at home.

17. Go to your favorite restaurant for dessert. Bring a child's baby book or your wedding album and relive some memories together.

18. Throw a party commemorating your spouse's graduation date.

19. Get the children together and make a "Why I Love Mom" and "Why I Love Dad" book, complete with text and illustrations.

20. Take your spouse out for an afternoon spent in her favorite store. Note the items under $20.00 she likes best. Return to the store the next day and buy one of those items as a gift.

Friendship, planning, surprises, and tapping into each other's creativity are all-important aspects of romance, but before we close this chapter, we need to sound one caution. Let's take a brief look at something that can kill a romantic experience faster than a duck can jump on a June bug.

Putting Romance in the Deep Freeze

Imagine the following scene. A man and woman are casually strolling arm in arm along a beautiful white sand beach. The waves gently wash ashore, and the sea-gulls dart back and forth overhead. A full moon glimmers in the night sky, and the sand seems like an endless strand of silver dust. It's a romantic ending to a perfect day, until . . .

If you look more closely, you will see the look on her face. It isn't one of peace and love. It's one of frustration and anger. Why? The setting is all right, but something he did is all wrong.

Ten minutes before, she told him she wanted to take a quiet walk on the beach and talk. He agreed to the walk which excited her—but he destroyed the romantic setting when he held her hand with one hand, and his fishing pole in the other.

"Hey, I've been casting for years," he told her. "I can talk and fish at the same time, *no problem!*"

This man broke two cardinal rules of romance. *1. Make sure the romantic activity you're involved in receives your full, undivided attention. 2. Make sure you're doing the activity for her best interests, not yours.*

Any time I send Norma flowers, or give her a card, or do something special, I'm saying, "I love you." At the moment it's spontaneous and unclouded by hidden motives, but I can quickly ruin it for her. All I have to do is ask a favor or tell her about my plans for fishing with the guys that weekend, or intimate that what I've done "deserves" a romantic response, and it's as if I walked into the house saying, "Gee, honey . . . you're sure looking bad today."

We've seen several ways in which the courtship aura can remain in a marriage. First, romance doesn't just happen "naturally" in a marriage; it's not simply an extension of physical intimacy. It takes work! Second, the winning recipe for romance is found in developing a friendship centered on shared interests—and carefully planned. Third, by using surprise, spontaneity, and creativity in romance, we can celebrate those special moments that bond us in a meaningful way. Finally, we need to make sure we give our full, undivided attention to our loved one during a romantic time. Each of these suggestions on keeping the courtship alive in our marriage can help to insure that this important area of our lives blossoms like flowers after a spring rain.

The key to being romantic, then, is to concentrate on being *relational*! When that happens, and your spouse truly senses you desire a deep, intimate friendship, then the stage is set to enjoy the wonderful pleasures of physical intimacy. Let's now examine what makes the sexual union meaningful and fulfilling for both the husband and the wife.

11

Sex Is Much More Than Physical Intimacy

Without question, one of the most interesting topics to both men and women is sex. But does physical intimacy mean the same to a man as it does to a woman? Hardly.

What is the basic physical need of a man? In most cases, the sexual act, and then, coming in a distant second, nonsexual touching. What is the basic physical need of a woman? Meaningful communication, nonsexual touching, and then sex.

We've looked at three ways in which a man or woman can nurture a marriage and see it bloom and grow. Each one is an important part of establishing a successful relationship—but the three are incomplete without a fourth. Within the confines of marriage, God has provided a way to meet an important need in a man and woman's life—that of physical intimacy.

Meeting Each Other's Needs

Numerous studies have shown that 70 to 80 percent of a woman's physical need is simply to be touched and held.[1] Just the opposite is true for a man, especially during the first several years of marriage. For most men, until they move into their late thirties, you could paint a big "T" on their T-shirt. The "T" could represent the sex hormone "testosterone" which tends to drive a man sexually.

In laboratory studies, if researchers inject a female Rhesus monkey with the hormone testosterone, she will gather other female monkeys around her and try to reproduce. Then, once the hormone has worn off, she'll go back to her more natural behavior.

(Some men have heard about the effects of testosterone and driven straight to their local druggist to see if they can get a prescription for their wives. However, as a dangerous steroid, the physical side-effects would include her shaving and being able to out arm-wrestle her husband.)

Perhaps a word picture might help to explain the common difference between a man and a woman in the sexual area. When it comes to marital intimacy, men tend to be like microwave ovens—instantly ready to be turned on at any time, day or night, and also ready to hurry through the cooking experience. The average woman, however, is more like a crock-pot. She needs to warm up to the sexual experience and savor the process, and the thing that warms her up the most is a quality relationship.

To get an idea of your husband's sexual appetite, think about your own desire to eat. How often do you feel hungry when you're on a diet? If you're like most of us, it's three times a day —morning, afternoon, and night! The hunger drive hits a woman on a diet about as often as a man's sex drive naturally hits him— especially during the first years of marriage. That's why a man can slip into bed at 10 o'clock at night after not seeing his wife all day, reach over and touch her on the shoulder, and say, "What do you *think*?"

After a hard day at work, with the kids or both—and little or no meaningful relational time spent to prepare her—her response may well be:

"*What do I think*! You *animal.* Don't even *think* about what you're thinking!"

To most women, sex is much more than just an independent physical act. It's the culmination of a day filled with security, conversation, emotional and romantic experiences, and then, if all is right, sex. For the average man, you can reverse the order— or just skip everything that comes before sex!

In many ways, it's just as hard for the average male to initiate intimate conversations and plan romantic activities as it is for his wife to initiate sex. But these two different needs in the physical area can be met—in a fulfilling way—for both a man and a woman. This is true particularly if you're aware of several practical attitudes and actions that can help to fan passion's flame.

Meaningful Touching Outside the Bedroom
Can Help the Touching Inside

Recently I read of a survey conducted among several hundred women.[2] In it, nearly 70 percent of the women responding claimed that if they were never again involved in the sexual act with their husbands, they wouldn't complain a great deal. What they would strongly miss was not being touched, held, and caressed. Every area of a woman's life is affected if she's not touched and held by the most important people in her life. As we mentioned earlier, eight to ten meaningful touches a day is really a minimum requirement for a woman to stay emotionally and physically healthy.

One man I know took his wife's need for meaningful touches so seriously that it got him in real trouble. As he was lathering up in the shower, he realized he'd forgotten a towel. Opening the shower door, he made a mad dash for the linen closet in the hallway. As he opened the closet door, he looked and saw his wife standing at the far end of the hall in the kitchen.

An impulsive thought crossed his mind, and he decided he'd give his wife one of those "meaningful hugs" she needed—right in the kitchen—and with soap and water added. So without a stitch of clothing on and dripping wet, he ran down the length of the hallway and burst into the kitchen to give her a great big bear hug—and that's when he saw the neighbor lady sitting at the kitchen table.

Proper timing might need to be taken into account when giving meaningful touches, but they are certainly one important way to grow a strong physical relationship.

Learning to Put Problems at Arm's Length

Do you know what are the two *least* talked-about areas in most marriages? Death and sex. I'm not sure what the relationship is between these two subjects, but I do know many couples don't see anything humorous about either one. Unfortunately, the lack of communication about the physical side of marriage can add to the problems a couple may have—not subtract from them.

To have a healthy sexual relationship, a couple needs to have the freedom to talk about this often "out of bounds" area, the freedom to share their likes, dislikes, expectations, and frustrations. We know of one couple who used the "word picture" method we talked about in Chapter 9 to open up this sensitive area. The method resulted in their becoming closer than ever before.

Darryl was a pro football player on a championship team that wasn't in the habit of losing. Yet when it came to the sexual area of his relationship with his wife, he felt that they were always having a disappointing season. In particular, he was frustrated about how seldom she would respond to his advances—and the negative fallout that would result from his desires being blocked.

Finally, he became so frustrated he decided to come up with a word picture to explain his feelings. So, after being rebuffed again after watching her get ready for bed, and trying to initiate an intimate time, he sat next to her and shared his word picture.

"Honey, we have *got* to talk," he said.

"Do you know how I'm feeling about our sexual life? I feel as if every night we're playing the shell game. Do you know what I mean? It's the game where there are three cups placed in a row upside down on the dresser.

"Under one of those cups is a bean, and if I can just pick the cup that has the bean under it—you'll be in the mood and we'll share some 'you know what!' But the problem is, I *never* pick the right cup. I feel like every day when I'm at practice, you shuffle the cups all around, and no matter which one I pick when I come home, it's always the wrong one. What I want to know is when are you going to quit hiding the bean?"

Darryl sat back, confident that his word picture would run loose through her mind like an all-pro running back. Certainly now that she understood his feelings, his word picture would score a touchdown for his desires. Undoubtedly, it would result in nonstop "availability" on her part. The only problem was that two can play at word pictures, and the one she shared with him in response reversed fields and scored points for her team.

"Darryl, since you asked, let me tell you the reason why we end up playing the shell game most nights. Let's say I'm your favorite fishing reel." Susan instantly had Darryl's interest when she mentioned fishing—one of his favorite activities in life.

"When we were first married, I felt that I was in beautiful shape, having come right from the factory and being wrapped up in a gift box. As soon as we were married, however, you threw me an old rod you had and took me right out and fished me in salt water. Then when you got home, you never washed me off or took care of me.

"When you first got me, you could cast me a mile because my line wasn't all knotted up, and I was oiled and well taken care of. But over the years with the way you've treated me, the reel has gotten salt-corroded and rusted, the line is all frayed, and the eyelets on the fishing rod are all bent and twisted. Now, whenever you have the impulse, you take me out of the corner of the garage where you've thrown me, and without ever taking care of me, expect me to cast as if I'm brand new.

"Can you see now why all you get is knots and backlashes when you try to cast me?"

Her husband answered, "Well, what in the world can I do?"

"You can either leave me in the garage and get the kind of response you're getting now, or you can fix me," she said. "Honey, if you would hold me and listen to me and quit lecturing me when I ask you a question—it would help me respond like a reel with a brand-new line and new eyelets."

That night, Darryl walked into a word picture that hit him harder than an NFL linebacker. For the first time he was able to "see" what the problem was in their sexual relationship in a way that he could understand.

> *Meaningful touching outside the bedroom can light sparks in a marriage, and meaningful communication can fan the flames.*

They ended up on the back porch talking for hours about a "fishing reel." But in actuality, they were talking about the most intimate area of their marriage. Darryl learned what it would take to "maintain" Susan in a way that could actually make her excited about responding to him. On the other hand, she was able to understand how frustrating the "games" they were playing by not talking about this very important area were.

As an unexpected bonus, they both ended up sharing one of the most romantic evenings in months. Why? Because a word picture can help to take even the most difficult subject and put it at arm's length where it can be more easily seen and talked about.

Like many couples, Darryl and Susan were so close to their problems, they couldn't see the forest for the trees. What a word picture did for them was to take them up in a helicopter to where they could get their bearings, see where they first went off the trail, and find the right pathway back to sexual intimacy.

Meaningful touching outside the bedroom can light sparks in a marriage, and meaningful communication can fan the flames. If a couple cares enough to explain their needs, frustrations, and enjoyments to one another, it can help to turn their relationship around. But there's still more that a couple can do.

Purifying Our Character
Increases the Passion Level in a Home

What do you think our "lovesick" society would say is the greatest "love story" ever told? Clark Gable and Vivian Leigh in *Gone with the Wind* during the '30s? Humphrey Bogart and Ingrid Bergman in *Casablanca* during the '40s? Burt Lancaster and Deborah Kerr in *From Here to Eternity* in the '50s? Ali McGraw and Ryan O'Neal in *Love Story* during the '60s? Barbra Streisand and Robert Redford in *The Way We Were* during the '70s? Or Kelly McGillis and Tom Cruise in *Top Gun* in the '80s?

Actually none of these would be right (or even close!). The greatest love story of all times is recorded right in the Scriptures. In fact if junior high kids realized that an entire book in the Bible talks specifically and explicitly about romance, sex, and intimacy, they'd turn to it in droves. (Of course, they would have to understand a little bit about Hebrew poetry.)

How do we know this love story is the greatest? Because we're told so in the title of the book. This book announces itself as "The Song of Songs" in bold letters. For a reader of Hebrew, something significant stands out. When biblical writers wanted to address something as "the very best, the highest, without equal," they repeated it. In other words, that's why we read statements like "the King of kings" and "the Lord of lords!" in reference to Christ. He is the King above all kings and the Lord without equal.

The title's repetition of the words, "The Song of Songs," then, tells us that this is it. It's the greatest love story of all times. It begins with a strong statement of passion.

"Let him kiss me with the kisses of his mouth!" Solomon's bride says to him in the first full verse of the book. For observant readers, that's *her* initiating an intimate response and *her* asking for him to kiss her—repeatedly!

For every man who was ready to inject his wife with testosterone, here is an example of a woman who didn't need any artificial prompting to want to kiss her husband. Interested in what prompted those words of passion from Solomon's bride?

If we look at the very next verse, we're given the reason—and it might surprise us. She tells us that it wasn't his charm or his good looks; it wasn't the expensive cologne or clothes he could afford to wear as the king; it wasn't even his prestige and power. What made his bride responsive to him was his character (Song of Songs 1:3). Her passion came as a direct reflection of the positive qualities in his life.

"May he kiss me with the kisses of his mouth. . . . *For your name is like purified oil,*" she tells him.

Let's not confuse our modern-day techniques for purifying oil with the way it was done in biblical times. The process this woman is picturing involved taking several trays of different size rocks and layering them from large rocks to the smallest pebbles. By the time oil had dripped through all those layers of rocks and pebbles, all the impurities had been filtered out and only "purified" oil remained. To this bride, Solomon's life, his "name," reflected that same process of purification. All the rough edges of indifference and insensitivity had been filtered out, and his wisdom and character reflected purity of "name" and purpose.

What Solomon's wife is telling us is a truth about marital passion. The more purified my character, the more attractive I am to my spouse—and the more responsive she'll be to me as a result. Time and again I've seen this principle working in the relationships of people—for good or for bad.

I remember the case of a man who lost his job with an insurance agency primarily because he wouldn't do something that was clearly illegal. He knew if he refused to comply with the wishes of his superiors, he'd be instantly fired—but he also knew he'd lose far more if he lied.

On the day before he went in to his boss to tell him he couldn't "cooperate," he went home and told his family about what he had to do. Dinner got cold that night as he made it clear to his wife and daughters that losing his job could very well mean they would lose their house as well.

This living object lesson of standing up for the truth distinctly marked his daughters and actually brought the family even closer together in the weeks that followed. But the response from his wife startled him. Even though his dinner got cold that night, her response to him sexually was the warmest, most romantic that he'd ever experienced in fourteen years of marriage. He was totally shocked, but Solomon wouldn't have been. This man's wife had seen her husband's character ring true as a bell, and that promoted far more passion than any flowers or gifts could ever do.

Before we move on, there is another side to this principle to consider. For those who want to see the romantic spark doused with buckets of cold water—all it takes is exposing major impurities in one's character. I remember the case of another person who did this, and it came very close to ruining his marriage.

Bill was a social climber who had to have the best clothes and the best car—but he couldn't afford either. It's not that he didn't make money, it's just that he didn't make nearly as much as he spent. One day, that dishonoring fact came crashing down on his wife.

He and his wife were both working, in large part so that the children could attend an excellent Christian school nearby. With the fall semester beginning, she handed him her endorsed paycheck to cover the beginning cost of their tuition. Without telling her, he cashed the check and spent it on a "need" he had for a new suit.

He fully intended to "rob Peter to pay Paul" and pay the tuition from another account before anyone else was the wiser—but Peter came up broke. That's when the call from the school came to his wife's office. It landed like a bombshell.

It was the school secretary on the phone. Regretfully she informed the wife that her children wouldn't be able to attend class any more until their tuition was paid. The wife confronted her husband when he got home. He lied at first, still trying to cover his tell-tale tracks. Then he made up another lie to cover the first one. Soon his character looked so full of impurities to her that she didn't even want to see him—much less touch him in love. It took months of counseling about his spending problems and re-establishing a track-record of trust before she began to respond to him physically again.

The moral of the story? Our romantic relationship may never be called the "Song of Songs," but we can still sing the chorus with gusto. And a clear stanza from that very helpful song reads, "If you want to raise the passion level in your marriage— increase the purity of your character."

Passion Grows Where a National Average Doesn't

We've all read reports in newspapers or magazines that give an "average number of times" that the "average" couple has sexual relations each day/week/month/year/ or decade. I'm not really sure what the purpose of such averages are, except to increase the counseling rate.

Too many couples who struggle sexually let a phantom national average dictate their loving response. One or both spouses can be so busy chasing after a national average that they forget that the "goal" they're working so hard to achieve is just that— average.

How should couples interpret such figures? Frankly, I recommend that they don't keep track of them at all. In a normal marriage, there will be times of high sexual activity, and periods where it is very low. Trying to keep up with someone else's idea of what "average" is, is an invitation to sexual frustration, not sexual satisfaction.

What's the best marriage guide? The Owner's manual on wise living, namely the Bible. First Corinthians 7:3–5 gives us a healthy "average" to shoot for: "The husband should fulfill his marital duty to his wife, and likewise the wife to her husband. The wife's body does not belong to her alone but also to her husband. In the same way, the husband's body does not belong to him alone but also to his wife."

In other words, a desire to respond to each other in love and a consistent willingness to meet each other's legitimate needs is the best advice on when to be sexually intimate. Don't let anyone set a loving "schedule" for you from a book or newspaper. Look to the Book for the best advice on timing—and on increasing intimacy as well.

Keep "Performance" on the
Stage and out of the Bedroom

There are two words that work well on the playing field but are absolute killers in the bedroom. What are they? *Performance anxiety.*

The Diagnostic Statistical Manual, Volume III, is an encyclopedia of psychological dysfunctions. In fact, it lists almost 200 pages of possible sexual problems. Do you know what one of the primary "treatment choices" is for all but a handful of these many disorders? "*Decrease* performance anxiety." In other words, if you can get acting and unrealistic expectations out of the bedroom, you can erase almost every sexual dysfunction that doesn't have a physiological basis, and you decrease performance anxiety by lowering expectations to realistic levels, focusing on genuine love, and seeking to meet the *other person's* needs, comfort, and pleasure instead of your own.

Often a man who has performance anxiety is one who judges the quality of his marriage by his sexual prowess. If, in the normal course of a marriage, he experiences some frustration in his sexual performance, fear can set in, and he can lose all confidence in this area. On the other hand, if a woman "performs" her way through the "act of marriage" by faking her real feelings or responses, genuine intimacy can be a long-forgotten experience. Couples need to stay clear of performance anxiety if they want passion to occur—and not be a memory from the past.

In a way, the sexual side of a relationship can be a barometer to the status of the marriage. In other words, if a wife is not responding to her husband sexually, 99 times out of 100 you can find the reason in their emotional or spiritual relationship. Some men may say, "Forget all these 'relationship' reasons for our sexual problems—I just married a frigid woman."

If you're one of these men, I suggest you honestly check the temperature of your relationship—the security level, the conversation, the sensitivity and romance, and the meaningful touching apart from the sexual act. In reality, *less than three per cent of all women are organically nonorgasmic or truly "frigid."* Of course, I can just hear someone saying, "It figures. I've got one of those wives in the three per cent." If that's your attitude, this is where honor needs to comes in.

Love Does Not Dishonor . . .

Dishonoring words that come up around the sexual area act like red lights to an intimate response. Take the man who would comment on his wife's need to "lose weight" just as she undressed to get into bed. Usually it's the same man who couldn't understand why she was cold and unresponsive. Or what about the woman who "teased" her husband about his sexual endurance until they had a major problem in his responding at all?

Solomon's bride knew she was deeply loved by her husband, but still she says, "Do not stare at me because I am dark . . ." (Song of Songs 1:6). Ever since Adam and Eve hid their nakedness from God and each other, there has been a natural insecurity around the sexual act. That level of insecurity can be multiplied by ten with poorly timed or insensitive words, but it's not only words that can be dishonoring and result in lowered passion. Actions can speak louder and more powerfully in this area.

Not too long ago, a man approached me as I was walking out to my car after a seminar. I could tell he was nervous.

"Gary, could I ask you just one question before you leave?" It was pushing eleven o'clock at night, following the first session of our seminar.

"I didn't want to ask this in front of anyone else," he said. "That's why I didn't come up to you inside. You see, I have a problem in my marriage. For years I've been making my wife do something when we're making love that she has hated doing, and now it's gotten so bad, she doesn't want to have anything to do with me at all. *Gary, isn't my wife supposed to submit to me, or am I reading the Bible wrong?*"

The answers to his questions were yes and yes. Yes, the Bible does say that a woman is to place herself under the loving leadership of her husband, and yes, he was reading the Bible wrong. Nowhere does it say that "submission" gives a man (or woman) the right to make a spouse do something they feel is wrong or terribly "dishonoring"—just to meet a selfish need.

I know that there are books written by Christian leaders who say that basically anything is legal in the bedroom, but I would have to disagree. As we discussed in Chapter 2, at the heart of love is a decision to honor a person—to count him or her as incredibly valuable. Forcing my wife to violate her conscience to please my sexual appetite is absolutely wrong and an invitation to sexual problems.

Regardless of the "no holds barred" pictures of pornography that are painted throughout our culture as being "acceptable," some forms of sexual behavior are dishonoring. To ask a spouse to perform a sexual act that is wrong or repulsive to him or her is to show at least a degree of insensitivity or even a lack of love.

Being "one flesh" in a marriage is a wonderful gift of a happy marriage. But it's only one part of a successful relationship. Security, meaningful communication, emotional and romantic times . . . and physical intimacy go together like pieces of a puzzle to make a nearly complete picture of a fulfilling relationship. As we'll see in the last two chapters of this book, there is still a "missing piece" when it comes to a marriage of true oneness. If a marriage is to really reach its peak, a couple must learn how to tap into the *only consistent power source* for keeping their love alive through each season of life. But before we turn to this most important aspect of intimacy, let's look at one final way to build a close-knit family.

12

Discovering the Secret to a Close-Knit Family

Not long ago, John and I were doing our "Love Is a Decision" seminar right in our hometown of Phoenix, Arizona. Whenever they can, my family makes it a point to attend the seminar, so I wasn't surprised when my oldest son, Greg, told me he was coming. What did surprise me, however, was a special request he made.

"Dad," he asked, "could I take about five minutes and share something I think is really important for the parents to hear?"

Gulp! I was honored that Greg would ask, but I also knew all too well that he is the family clown. With his light-hearted nature, he is basically capable of doing or saying anything once he gets in front of an audience. Now he'd be in front of almost a thousand people, and the possibilities for disaster were endless. Then again, how often does your son ask to join you at a family conference? So I readily agreed.

Just for safe-keeping, I did schedule his five minutes during the afternoon of the second day. That way I figured if he did say something off the wall, it would come after a day and a half of positive input from Dr. Trent and myself.

As the time grew near for him to speak, I'll have to admit I became a little nervous. *They're about to hear some inside stories about the Smalley family,* I remember thinking to myself.

Greg began by saying, "I just want you to know what a privilege it is to be here with my Dad and to share in this seminar. I really enjoy being with him during times like this, *because it's one of the few times he's sober* . . . ."

The audience roared, and of course I thought, *Yep, I shot myself in the foot all right. What's this son of mine going to say next?*

"No, no," Greg laughed, "I'm kidding. My Dad doesn't even drink."

Then he said, "I want to share with you parents for a moment." I had been talking to these people for almost two days, and for the most part they had stayed right with me. When my son began to talk, however, I could see people actually leaning forward to hear what he was going to say.

"I want to encourage you to make every effort to become best friends with your kids—and there's an important reason why. I know firsthand that it can make a big difference in their lives as they get older.

"I'm in college now, and there's temptation everywhere. I've seen many of my friends go to other people they know on campus for advice on sex, drugs, cheating, you name it! And the suggestions they are getting would make your blood turn cold. It's like the blind leading the blind! In many cases, I know why they're going to friends and getting bad advice. It's because very few of them feel that they can go to their parents to ask the hard questions.

"That seems odd to me, because I've always been able to talk to Mom and Dad. Sometimes, I'll call them at two in the morning from school to talk about something I'm struggling with. I'm never afraid to wake them up because I know they really love me, and they want to listen to what's happening in my life.

"If I wasn't confident in their friendship, I would not have been able to call them—and I know I wouldn't be open to their counsel. I can assure you that the advice you give your children will be far wiser than most of what they'll hear from people in their dorms at school. So, please, to make sure they'll listen to you when the time comes . . . do what it takes today to build a strong friendship with your children when they're young, so that they'll *want* to come to you when they're older. . . ."

I've been speaking for years, but I can't think of a time when I've grabbed an audience as Greg did that afternoon. I also don't know when I've ever been more proud of him or more humbled to be his father.

Greg struck a chord on what is one of the most crucial factors in developing and maintaining a loving relationship: *learning to be best friends with your children.* At its heart, a close-knit family is one that respects and honors each member and experiences a deep bond of intimacy.

Almost nothing strengthens a husband and wife's relationship more than when the whole family is united and best friends. The question is, "How does a family take on that kind of personality on a consistent basis?"

What's the Secret to a Close-Knit Family?

Years ago, when our kids were little, I started speaking at family retreats across the country. As I spoke, I'd pick out families who looked happy and seemed to respond well to each other. When I had the opportunity, I'd approach the husband and wife with several questions.

First, I'd ask, "You seem to enjoy each other so much and have a real love for one another! What do you think is the most important thing you do as a family that makes you so close?"

Almost without exception, each family I interviewed said, "We've made a commitment to spend quality *and* quantity time together regularly. We have separate interests, but we make sure we do things together as a family on a regular basis."

Then I'd ask, "What's the one thing you do more than any other that you feel bonds you together?" Time and time again, I'd hear an answer that I simply couldn't believe. What was the common denominator of almost every one of these "successful" families? *Camping!*

At that time, Norma and I had never camped together— by choice. But since learning this secret, we've camped together for over fifteen years. That gives me some authority to speak on the subject, and I can say with absolute conviction— camping is *not* the secret. Before I let our noncamping friends off the hook, though, I do need to say that camping is still the best method I know to *find* the real secret to a close-knit family. You'll see what I mean by looking at our very first camping experience.

Baptism by Lightning

The evidence became overwhelming—we needed to go camping. The kids were small, but old enough to travel, so we decided to give it a try. We bought a tiny, second-hand pop-up tent-trailer, packed our gear, and sped off into the sunset.

We had spent a few nights sleeping in our driveway to "test out" the trailer, but our first night of camping out was in Kentucky. There we discovered a beautiful campground with pine trees everywhere. We set up camp under the shade of the largest pine we could find. That night we built a fire, cooked hot dogs, roasted marshmallows, and had a great time together.

Soon after dark the kids fell asleep in the camper, leaving Norma and me alone to talk the evening away by a nice crackling fire. Finally, we called it a night and crawled inside with the kids. We lay there, peaceful and content. For the life of me, I couldn't think what it was that had kept me from the wonders of camping all these years—but I was soon to find out!

Without any announcement, the wind began to blow steadily. Before long, a row of dark clouds marched overhead, and a gentle rain began to fall softly on the roof. Still, it was only a tranquil "pitter-patter" on the pop-up trailer. I settled back to smell the wonderful fresh scent of rain on a summer's night, and to listen to the soothing lullaby that would send us into dreamland. . . .

Then without warning, Wham! The gentle shower turned into a violent storm. The rain began to come down in sheets, and the wind whipped up to gale force levels. Our little camper, once seemingly anchored on firm ground, began to shake and sway like a break-dancer on television. Within moments, the rain was coming down so hard that it soaked through the seams of the canvas roof and began leaking inside the trailer.

Far worse than the rain was what followed. "Round two" of the storm seemed to throw all its punches at once. Monumental lightning blasts crashed and roared all around us for a solid hour. Each bolt that darted from the sky lit up the night like a Fourth of July fireworks display. The first "near miss" lightning strike instantly blew out all the campground lights, leaving us alternating between blinding flashes of lightning and pitch-black, inky darkness.

About half-way through the thunder storm, Norma and I grabbed each other's hands. Finally, she whispered to me what we both had been fearing, "Do you think we're going to blow over?"

Knowing it was my job to remain calm and relax her, I said, "Naaaa . . . not a chance!" Truthfully, I didn't think we'd blow over. *I thought we were going to blow up!*

It's amazing what kind of thoughts go through your mind at a moment like that. I couldn't help thinking . . . *This is it! We're going home to be with the Lord tonight. When was the last time I told the kids I loved them? Who's going to take care of the dog when we don't get back? I wonder who they'll interview for my position at work?* I just knew that any moment, our shiny metal trailer was going to act like Ben Franklin's key on his kite and draw the next lightning blot right down on top of our heads.

Fortunately, our portable "lightning rod" didn't attract any shocking attention, and we made it through the night with little more than a lack of sleep and rain-soaked sleeping bags. Still the memories of that experience continue as vivid as the night it happened.

> *T*he real secret to becoming a close-knit family is shared experiences that turn into shared trials.

Fortunately, not all our camping experiences have been as harrowing as that first one. After we'd gotten a few trips under our belt, a funny thing happened. Just like the couples we'd interviewed, we began to see a deepening bond developing in our home. Why?

Knitting Hearts Together

Going through harrowing experiences as a family draws people together like virtually nothing else. In other words, the real secret to becoming a close-knit family is *shared experiences that turn into shared trials.*

Have you ever noticed the way grown men on a football team will suddenly act like grade school kids, running around screaming and hugging each other, after a close, come-from-behind victory? Or have you ever stood at the Vietnam Memorial in Washington, D.C., and seen the closeness that veterans have there with one another after having gone through the horrors of war? The link people in those situations share is an inseparable relationship, forged from a common experience that stands the test of time.

I can think of one "trying" experience in particular that has marked my life forever—and my family's.

When our third child, Michael, was born, I have to admit I was a little upset. As terrible as it sounds, I wasn't sure I wanted another child. So, initially, I was ambivalent toward him and irritated with Norma for "talking" me into having another child.

I knew my attitude was dead wrong, but honestly, it was the way I felt at the time. During the first three years of his life, I just wasn't as close to Mike as I should have been. I wanted to feel close to him, at times I desperately tried, but nothing I did seemed to spark the emotional fires—that is until the spark of life almost went out of his life.

God's Mercy Creates an
Unforgettable Bonding Memory

We were moving to Texas, enroute from Chicago, when Mike was a little over three years old. We had been traveling all day when we decided to spend the night at a motel—with a swimming pool.

It had been a long summer's day with five people stuffed into a tiny car, and the minute the kids spotted the shimmering water, they went crazy. I had to admit the water looked pretty good to me, too. We quickly checked in, dumped our bags in the rooms, and headed for the pool.

Norma took a quick dip and then curled up on a pool-side lounge chair with a *Good Housekeeping* magazine. In no time, the rest of us were in the water, really enjoying ourselves. Kari and Greg were old enough to swim, but Michael needed a small, round inner tube to keep him afloat.

After making sure he was "seaworthy" I turned my attention to the other two, who were screaming for me to play "toss me up," a game where I threw them up in the air and let them land in the water. After a few minutes with them, I looked back over my shoulder to see how our youngest was doing.

I saw the tube floating, but I didn't see Michael. At first, I couldn't believe my eyes. I thought Norma must have gotten him out of the water. Then I saw his tiny little body lying at the bottom of the pool. The only thing moving was his blond hair waving in the water. Instantly I swam underwater, grabbing him in my arms. When we broke the surface, his eyes were dilated, and he was coughing and sputtering.

When I got him on the deck, I began shaking him to get the water out of his lungs. In retrospect, Mike was probably in more danger from me trying to help him than he ever was on the bottom of the pool! After a couple of minutes he was back to normal, with all of us doting over him like a proud mother over a new baby.

When I first looked over and saw my son lying on the bottom of the pool, I was sure we'd lost Michael. During that instantaneous moment of emotion, something took place between us that has never left our relationship. There's something about seeing your three-foot-high son in five feet of water—knowing each second he's down there more life is draining out of him—that melts your hearts together like nothing else. That is, unless it's his first words after nearly drowning.

I'll never forget what Michael said to me when he was finally fully awake and breathing. "Daddy," he said looking at me with tears in his eyes, "I could see your legs, but I couldn't reach you!"

Instantly, my feelings of ambivalence toward my son were gone. I felt closer to him than ever before—and that bond has never been broken.

It was nearly a tragic mistake on my part that I had not kept a closer eye on Michael. As we realize now, it was God's grace that allowed me to go through that traumatic experience with my son. It shook me out of my passive indifference and replaced it with a special love for a very unique and valuable son. Michael has been, is, and always will be a living memorial of God's mercy to me. Each time any of our family brings up that harrowing experience, it unites our hearts in a bond of love and commitment.

Fast-Drying Bonds of Love

None of us would plan disasters just to make our family close knit. If your family is like mine, though, *you don't have to plan them*. They just happen! Because you never know for sure when the next one's coming, you've automatically got the perfect recipe for a "crazy glue" mixture that's perfect for family bonding.

"Crazy glue" experiences are what bonds us to one another in the midst of unexpected crisis. When we're forced by circumstance to go through something trying with another person, the crazy glue gets set in place, and once it hardens the result can be life-changing.

Most of the time, being in the middle of a crisis doesn't find us saying, "Isn't this great! We're all feeling so close right now!" Normally, we're at each other's throats saying things that aren't nearly so positive. The secret is how we'll feel later.

In most cases it takes about three weeks for the "glue" of a shared crisis to set and permanent bonding to take place. Once set, though, it's usually so tight that virtually nothing can tear the memory apart. Let me give you a recent example of a family experience that has "stuck" like glue to our family's emotions.

Famous Last Words: "Trust Me"

We live in a small patio-home in a private subdivision in Phoenix. It's so private, in fact, that the homeowners' association even owns the streets! When Michael was fourteen, he asked if he could drive the car down the street a few houses and pick up some wood we could burn in our fireplace.

Since we lived on a private road, I didn't see any harm in it, so I gave him the go-ahead. But when Norma found out what I'd done, she was beside herself.

"Norma, relax," I said. "This is a private road. It's no problem. *Trust me.*"

A few moments later, we heard a tremendous "BANG!!!" Norma screamed and ran outside, with me just a step behind. When we got there, what we saw looked like something out of the new Disneyland-MGM Studio's theme park.

There was our van, looking as if the garage door had suddenly come to life and attacked it. When Mike started to pull into the driveway, he had accidentally pushed on the accelerator, not the brake. Ramming our van into the garage door made it look like a crumpled soda can. Because of poor judgment on my part, we had a pug-nosed van, one hysterical mother worried if her son was hurt, and one angry father ready to hurt his son's posterior if the accident hadn't hurt him. But there's more.

We'd only recently converted the garage into Greg's bedroom, and "typically," he was asleep inside at the time of the accident. When the van hit the garage door, it knocked a mounted fish off the wall, right onto Greg's head! Scared to death, he thought a massive earthquake had just hit Phoenix, so he jumped up and ran out of the house thinking the apocalypse had come.

At that moment, there was very little bonding going on around the Smalley household. Let's just say that as the neighbors began gathering to view the scene, not one of us felt like laughing. Several weeks later, though, something miraculous happened.

While we never thought it possible during the midst of our "van" crisis, in three weeks time we'd all calmed down, and the garage door was fixed. Today, nearly a year later, it's one of the funniest stories we re-live with each other. Who'd have thought that a smashed garage door could have provided some of the best "crazy glue" for bonding a close-knit family that we've ever experienced? The Smalley family almanac is full of stories that have "crazy glued" us together. It's no wonder we're close.

To make sure the glue sets properly in a home, it's important to remember one thing: *During difficult times, it's vital not to do or say anything that will close the spirit of others.*[1] Harsh words and calloused actions in the heat of battle are the quickest way to dilute the glue.

That afternoon, I realized I had said several things in anger to Michael that I shouldn't have, and I had to apologize to him and ask his forgiveness. It's best when level heads and open hearts work together to cement family "disasters" into positive family memories that can hold you together forever.

Once you know the "stick 'em" power of a well-handled disaster, minor family crises can actually become welcome visitors in your home. While they may knock down the door like an unwelcomed guest at first, once the crisis leaves there is an opportunity for stronger, more intimate relationships.

How do I know this for a fact? Namely, because the same principle that helps draw a family together during times of trial, works in our bonding with our Heavenly Father.

Glued to the Father

One of the most amazing things I've learned is that the same bonding that happens to families in a crisis can happen in our relationship with God when a person of faith goes through trying times.

Have you ever been through a struggle and had to depend totally on the Lord? There's nothing like the helplessness of feeling there's no one on earth to turn to. As Christians, we may often *feel* that way, but the reality is that we can always turn to the most powerful, influential Person in the whole universe and totally depend on Him. Often He allows us to experience that kind of loneliness and desperation so we'll learn lessons about His great love and faithfulness we wouldn't discover otherwise.

Walking through those valleys, you can feel a bonding with God that the "good times" just can't produce. Lessons learned about His loyal love are what inspired David to write: "The Lord is my shepherd, I shall not want. . . . *though I walk through the valley of the shadow of death,* I will fear no evil; for thou art with me . . . " (Psalm 23:1,4 KJV, italics mine). Talk about bonding! David was a man whose heart cleaved to God's because he had faced the fires and yet God saw him through.

In the same way, when disastrous things happen to each of us, we can respond in thankfulness to Him, confident the experience will make us more trusting of Him. (This principle of looking to God to find value in trials is so important, we will take an entire chapter to talk about it.)

Making positive memories out of trying times is probably one of the most powerful ways to develop a friendship I know of today. Remember when Greg stood up in front of several hundred parents and urged them to become "best friends" with their children? Reflecting on past memories is one way to do it. This is especially true if you've suffered through some family crisis that you can look back on and laugh about. This very kind of disaster was one of the worst—but funniest—experiences of my life.

Just Hanging Around

It happened a few months before Christmas. Norma asked me what I wanted her to give me that year. I told her I'd been thinking about a pair of inversion boots, the kind you buckle yourself into and then use to hang upside down to stretch out all your muscles. I told her that before I made the request official, I wanted to try something first.

Norma left for the grocery store, and, thinking this was as good a time as any to try the "invention" out, I went to the garage. I drilled some holes in an old pair of boots, placed a metal hook in each one, and put them on. Then I got out my ladder, climbed up and hung myself upside down from my son's chinning bar. Actually the boots worked fine—my muscles certainly felt as if they were being stretched like never before. But I soon realized I had created a major problem with my new invention.

The problem was, now that I was upside down—hooked to the chin-up bar—I couldn't get down! I was stuck! What's worse, I didn't have enough strength to reach up and loosen the boots to free myself. To top things off, nobody was around. I was left to hang there helplessly like a side of beef in a meat freezer. I had visions of heart failure, and Norma opening the garage door, seeing me, and thinking, *Gary sure chose a weird way to commit suicide!*

The person who finally found me was Greg, the family clown! He had heard my cries for help, opened the door, saw me hanging there, and fell on the ground howling like a hyena.

There I dangled. Dear old Dad. The one who helped to change his diapers, who played ball with him in the park for countless hours, who worked long, hard hours to put food in his mouth and clothes on his back; and all he could do was laugh while I was dying!

Finally, Kari came in and urged Greg up off the floor and tried to help me. Even together, however, they were not strong enough to get me down. By this time, I knew I was going to die. I knew I was about to have a stroke that would finish me. Norma would have to fight the insurance company for years to prove that my death wasn't "suspicious."

At long last, Kari went to get some scissors and cut the shoe strings on my boots. This was certainly helpful in getting me out of the boots, but what they had failed to do was move the ladder I'd used. As a result, I fell onto it and onto the concrete floor and cut and bruised by head and hip.

The moment I hit the floor, the kids scattered—and for good reason. I can assure you, if I had been able to move just then, I would have "laid hands" on them!

It's been several years since my "upside down" adventure, and just like our camping trips, the "crazy glue" of that shared trial has made this story one of our favorite family memories. It was a crisis that everyone in my family enjoyed, even me—after I got over the humiliation.

I have to be honest, though. That's not the end of the story. Two years later Mike and I were visiting some friends in a beautiful home in Seattle. I noticed they had a workout room with a *real* pair of inversion boots.

You know the rest of the story. I got stuck *again*. This time Mike got to do the honors of helping me down. Years after I've gone to be with the Lord, I'm sure my children and *their* children will still get together and talk—and yes, laugh—about "Dad and his boots."

Please Write on Our Walls

To add even more "bonding" glue to your memories, you can actually plan humorous things around your house that will build relationships and create happy times for your whole family as well. We know of a radio talk show host in our city who was a master at creating fun-bonding times when his children were young.

For example, when his son turned ten, he invited all the neighborhood kids over for the party—but not just *any* birthday party. He had saved for months and spent a small fortune in supplying an incredible surprise. Namely, 800 cream pies that he'd ordered for the biggest birthday pie fight that Phoenix has probably ever seen.

His son is grown now, but still recalls that party as one of the greatest highlights of his childhood—and almost every kid who participated does as well. It was terrific fun for everyone, and it created a special bond between father and son that still holds strong today. Still, that's not the extent of this creative man's talents.

As a radio celebrity, he was always being given "promotional" T-shirts when he would do commercials or "live" broadcasts. Even with giving many away to the Salvation Army, his shirt drawer soon began to bulge, and he came up with a creative idea.

When his kids were grade-school age, about once a month he'd pull out an old T-shirt that was ready for the trash (or one he'd been given that he knew he'd never wear). Then when he saw all the kids were home, he'd walk through the house yelling, "*I hope no kids are listening!* I sure hope there aren't any aggressive kids in their rooms that want to be destructive today and tear a T-shirt off of me. Because this T-shirt has a hole in it, and I'm ready to throw it away. . . ."

No sooner had he finished speaking than doors would burst open all over the house and voices screaming with delight would echo down the halls. From everywhere, his four kids would dive all over him and tear this shirt to pieces. He loved it, and they loved him for it.

How about one more example of a creative dad who knows that letting kids occasionally experience something "out of the ordinary" can build lasting, loving memories?

In every home, what is one rule that is always established as soon as a child begins testing his fine-motor skills? That's right. "Don't write on the walls." Just as in everyone else's home, this man's kids also had to obey this rule—until he decided that he'd make one "marked" exception.

One day, he and his wife were struggling over how to redecorate the guest bathroom when he came up with a very creative idea. He called the kids in (after talking to his wife, of course) and told them that whenever they brought home a friend, that child could sign his or her name on one of the bathroom walls. Of course, the wall signing had to begin by having the children put their names in what may have become the largest autograph book in Arizona.

Every other wall in the house was still "off limits" to writing, but soon this guest bath became a focal point of the entire neighborhood. It has stayed that way even now that the kids are all grown and out of the house. Today, when this man's children bring people over to their parents' home, the bathroom is still the first place they visit to have them see or "sign" the wall.

You may not know of many people who spend part of every "family reunion" all jammed into a guest bathroom . . . but now you do. This family loves to gather and look at years' worth of happy memories captured in the names of grade school, high school, and college friends of the kids—and the "grown up kids" who are the parents' friends who also insist on signing the bathroom wall! One creative idea resulted in positive memories shouting from four walls that could have just held wallpaper.

Any kind of fun time you plan, even if it's just wrestling with your kids or playing leapfrog, is something that can bind you in special and significant ways. Don't let "tradition," or fatigue, or a busy schedule, steal all the fun from your family times. It's so important.

John and I have a very close friend named Bill Butterworth who is one of the most outstanding family conference speakers in the country.[2] Often, he asks his audiences this open-ended question: "If you could add anything to your home—what would it be?"

Do you know what answer he has received as the number 1 things many people wish they had more of inside their home? You guessed it—laughter.

Such an answer might surprise you—but then again, after reading this chapter, maybe not. In particular, it shouldn't shock Christians.

A very thought-provoking book came out a few years ago called *Desiring God.*[3] For many Christians, the Christian life can be something so cold and "humorless" it almost begs kids to look for a "cheerful heart" anywhere but in their home or church. Yet that should never be the case. In this author's book, he does a very good job of illustrating that "In the knowledge of God is fullness of joy." In other words, one clear hallmark of a Christian is a joyful life.

I fully realize that joking can sometimes be hurtful. Inappropriate humor can be sarcastic or disrespectful, but let's not leave joy out of a home if we want it to be marked as distinctively Christian. Your kids will always remember you for taking the time and creativity to add a sparkle of fun to the family—even if it costs you a T-shirt or two!

The Family That Decides Together, Bonds Together

Disasters can be great ways for family bonding to take place. For the faint of heart, however, it's also possible to plan times together as a family where neither hardship nor humor are the goals. These are special times for just being together, times that allow the opportunity for relationships to develop simply because you're with someone.

Family outings such as these generally don't happen without effort—particularly in our hectic, fast-paced world. So, the best thing to do is get the family together, talk about what you enjoy doing, and plan an event or activity everyone can enjoy.

But what if you're a group of "individuals" like my family and enjoy different activities? My family solved this situation by deciding to make it a priority to spend time together. That way, when it's time to plan a family activity, we're all open to talk about it.

"Okay, gang," I say, "it's time to plan this year's vacation.

On a scale of one to ten, ten being the best, what would be a ten for you this time?" Each member then has the opportunity to share what would be a "dream activity" for them.

Kari and Norma will usually answer, "A cute beach where I can lay out in the sun, and probably cute little shops nearby." Mike and Greg typically respond, "Water, fishing, snorkeling, rock-climbing—anything adventurous." Then we put our heads together and try to come up with a place or activity that will fit our budget and still accommodate everyone's wishes as much as possible.

Sometimes, we have to make compromises, but that can be a valuable time for our kids to learn the importance of considering each others' needs and wants ahead of their own (Philippians 2:3–8). It may take time to hammer out a solution, but our commitment to doing things together as a family is a great help in urging all of us to bend enough to arrive at a decision everyone is satisfied with.

In the last few years, as our kids have moved through the teenage years, there's been stiff competition between family time and their team sports, clubs, and church trips. Sometimes, we decide *as a family* that we're already busy enough. Still, we try to plan times together as much as our schedules will allow.

It's also important to make a family decision to spend time alone with each of your children. A few years ago Greg and I went to Eastern Europe together on a speaking trip. If you want to bond with someone, just go through a few communist road blocks together as they search and re-search every stitch of you and your luggage! We'll always have the memory of staying in homes where people literally risked their lives to meet and to talk about Christ.

Taking mini-mission trips to your local Salvation Army to serve Thanksgiving dinner or help the poor can be a tremendous bonding time, or plan several years in advance to save up to visit one of your church's missionaries in the field. You can encourage and help them with a specific project or need they may have. Instead of just letting the youth leader get the advantage of all the bonding that goes on during a missions trip, go with the kids as a sponsor yourself. Usually the church is in such need of "sponsors" they may even pick up your expenses to travel with the kids! You'll lose sleep and possibly some hearing (if they're allowed to bring their tape players), but you'll never lose the closeness that can come from trips like these.

We can all waste time on television and movies, but we'll never waste one minute of time giving our children a picture of what God is accomplishing throughout the world.

Let me say clearly that it's not the distance or expense that counts but the personal contact you have with your children during the event. Over the years, Kari and I have made a habit of going out together for yogurt to talk. The warm, intimate father-daughter conversations we've had will always be dear to me.

When Greg got up to share at our conference that day, it made me very aware—and very thankful for—of all the hours we'd spent camping as a family. In many ways, we'd collected a twofold benefit. All the trials and family experiences we had have produced a loving bond with the children stronger and deeper than Norma and I could ever imagine. They've done something else as well. They've also given Norma and me more love for each other—and more positive memories to hold on to now that the kids are grown and moving away.

Whether you do all your "camping" at the nearest Marriott or deep in the heart of the Colorado Rockies, there's no substitute for quality time as a couple—or a family. A close-knit home, like our relationship with our Christ, grows and deepens as we share together moments of trial, tenderness, and laughter.

Now, finally, what I think are the most important chapters await us. I'll never write on more important subjects than the ones you'll find in Chapters 13 and 14, for they provide the insights for us to gain the desire and inner strength to do all the honoring and loving things we've written about in this book. Without these two chapters, this book would be just another "skill-building" book, but in today's world with the pressures we face—skills aren't enough. You need to be able to fully tap into the only power source for a love that lasts—if you want your love to last a lifetime.

13

Finding Fulfillment: More Than Our Cup Can Hold

One morning, a wife was desperately trying to get her husband up for church. She kept pushing and shoving him, trying to get him out of bed. "Get up, George!" she said repeatedly. "We're going to be late for church again!"

Finally, he rolled over in frustration and said, "I told you last night, I am *not* going to church and that's final. Now let me go back to sleep."

"But George," she pleaded, "it's important for you to be there." Finally, she decided to use another approach. "Okay, George. Give me two good reasons why you shouldn't go to church."

"Fine," he said, "I'll give you two reasons. Number one, I don't *like* those people. And number two, they don't like *me* down there either. That's why I'm not going."

There was a long pause as his wife thought over his answer. Finally he spoke up and said, "If you feel it's really so important I go to church, why don't you give me two reasons why I should go?"

"George," she said, "first of all you know that the Bible says it's important for you to go to church, and second, *you're the pastor!*"

Like anyone, pastors can get discouraged. I spent a number of years working at several churches, and I know what it's like to be discouraged. In fact, I know what it's like not to want to get out of bed.

When We Feel Like Never
Coming out from under the Covers

When I was thirty-five years old, there was a time I was so depressed from what I thought life had "dealt" me, that all I wanted was to crawl under the covers and never show my face again.

I blamed all my miseries on this job, and that person, and those circumstances. I can remember being so discouraged over a heart-breaking ministry situation that I lay upstairs in my daughter Kari's room, not eating for almost four days. Each of my children would come up and try to encourage me, but I'd just tell them to go away—I didn't want to face anyone or anything. Norma did her best to break me out of the doldrums as well, but for days I stayed in a darkened room, alone with my misery.

Finally, I remember telling my wife that I had made an important decision. I was getting out of the ministry. I didn't want any part of all the stress and broken promises I'd faced, and I was going to leave and get into some other kind of work.

Norma turned to me and asked, "What would you do?" That's when I realized that I didn't *know* anything else to do. I had been trained for the ministry and nothing else. I really became depressed when I thought about that! In my mind, I was on a dead-end street with no hope of ever finding a pathway that would take me away from my troubles.

During this time, I remember doing something out of desperation that turned out to be the greatest thing that has ever happened to me in my life. This period of personal darkness was the worst experience that had ever happened to me, but it turned into the greatest thing I ever experienced because of what it taught me.

I learned one biblical principle that taught me several important things I may never have learned otherwise. I discovered how to use my emotions—even the negative ones—instead of just being used by them. I learned something that led me to lasting freedom from worry, fear, anxiety, hurt feelings, and depression. I also learned how to take all the negative things that happen to me and actually find positive good and deeper love for others within the trial (I'll focus on this in detail in the next chapter).

Most of all, that terrible experience taught me the secret to experiencing continuing fulfillment in life. This is the very thing any individual or couple must discover if their marriage is to stay strong over each season of life.

Looking for Love, Peace and Joy in All the Wrong Places

What did I learn that had such a dramatic impact on my life? For years before that period of depression, I had spent a lifetime looking to any number of things to give me a sense of significance and security. But I was trying to find the right things in the wrong places.

I learned that we all have similar goals in life. If our lives were like a cup, each one of us would love to have it filled with wisdom, love, joy, and peace. We'd like to have our lives overflow with positive emotions and genuine fulfillment in life. At a very early age, we all begin to look around for what we think can fill up our cup with these positive qualities.

Unfortunately, what most of us do is to look to one of three sources, or all three, to give us the fullness of life we really want. Yet like a mirage, they shimmer with fulfillment, but offer only dust to our souls.

Looking to People to Fill Our Cup

The first place many of us tend to look is toward people. We think to ourselves, *if I'm really going to have my needs met, I've got to have another person in my life.*

Take the average single woman in her early twenties or even thirties. Often, she'll spend hours thinking and dreaming of how that "special" someone will come into her life and fill up her cup. For some women who come from a difficult family background, their personal cup may have so little love, peace, and joy that they long to finally be filled up. So in these cases, there can be a tremendous desire for a "Mr. Wonderful" to come along who can make up for the empty arms and missing love they've experienced.

In her mind's eye, this woman can come home at day's end and find "him" waiting for her. She wants someone who would hold her gently in his arms and spend hours at night in intimate conversation. She is looking for someone who is thoughtful and kind—and can fill up her cup to overflowing.

Many women enter courtship this way, but before a woman has been married a year, panic begins to set in. That's because she begins to discover almost immediately that her husband is not only failing to fill her cup—but often this "special someone" is drilling little holes in her cup by his small, insensitive actions.

Now, in addition to her cup not getting fuller, she's starting to lose whatever positive feelings with which she came into the marriage! Many women have actually told me that they experienced feelings of emotionally "drying up" when they realized that their husband would never fill their cup.

Then something happens. A light can go on in this woman's eyes as she comes to a startling realization. It isn't a husband who fills her cup. *It must be children!* Of course! God's plan. Little children running around the house. So they have little babies running around the house, and soon they discover something that all children have the capacity to do. That is, children can drill *big* holes in the cup!

Now this woman may really face a problem. Neither her husband nor her children are always filling her cup. They can be frustrating and irritating and drain away as much—or more—emotional energy than they give.

For those who look elsewhere, they'll ultimately find the same frustration in any other relationship. Friends can be a tremendous source of help and encouragement at times, but even they can disappoint us over the long haul. We can look to them as the source of positive emotions, but at times they too can punch holes in our emotional lives.

Tragically, some people have even turned to an affair to try to "fill their cup." The sweet taste of stolen waters may seem to fill up one's life, but it's actually like drinking ice-cold salt water. The burning aftertaste of sin can burn huge holes in our cup and leave us emptier and more miserable than we ever imagined.[1]

If people aren't the source that fills up our lives with the positive emotions we want so much, what is?

Looking to Places as the Source of Fulfillment

"We need a home! That's it, we need a place with a beautiful view and trees that are the envy of the neighborhood. If only we had the right place to live, *then* our cup will be full." Then we get that special home and live in it for a short while, and suddenly things begin to go wrong. In part that's true because the bigger our home, the more things there are to fix when they break.

Norma and I live in Arizona where grass front lawns are an exception, but for a period of time we thought, *We need a place that can be an oasis in the desert. We need a house that has a beautiful lawn.* Surely *that* would help our cup be full. Once we got our lawn in, though, we then discovered we were chained to it just to keep it alive.

One year I didn't water it enough, and the grass all died. The next year, I watered it too much and killed the grass again. In fact, there were numerous times when I was tempted to bulldoze the entire yard and pave it over, I was so frustrated with it!

We can put in a swimming pool, a fireplace, or even buy a mountain cabin, and those "places" don't fulfill us. Why? In part because no matter how pretty or fulfilling places look, they don't fit inside our personal cup. Instead they all have sharp edges that cut holes in our lives. What's more, the *people* we share our special places with are the same ones who continue to drain our cup as well!

But if people *and* places don't fill up the deepest part of our lives, where do we turn to finally find love, peace, and joy?

Looking to Things for Fulfillment

How about more money so that we can buy more things? Many of us feel that if we just had more money, we'd be happier in life. But study after study of people who "strike it rich" show this isn't the case.

The more money we make, the more wisdom we must have to handle it. Now I know that many of us wouldn't mind having to come up with that kind of wisdom. But to get money we normally have to pay a personal price. Thomas Carlyle once said, "For every person who can handle prosperity, there are a hundred who can handle adversity." Money alone, and all the things it can bring, can't fill up our lives with the kind of living water we desperately want.

I've met people all over the country who have little money and are miserable. And I've also met those with lots of money who are miserable. I've known people who have mountain cabins and third cars and aren't fulfilled. And some people I know barely have bus fare, but they also feel empty inside.

Most people who depend on "things" to "fill up their cup" end up looking for the one "perfect" job that will be the ticket to all their dreams. All jobs have one thing in common—work! And work doesn't always keep our cup full. It can positively drain us in terms of the people we work with, the place where we do our work, the equipment we must use, and so on.

Some of us try all our lives to get a key to a certain washroom, or a parking space with our name on it. When we get it, however, what do we have? The answer to being filled with wisdom, love, peace, and joy? Hardly. Just the opposite is too often true.

Coming up Empty in Life

At some times in each one of our lives, we run headlong into an inescapable fact. Life is not fulfilling. It's actually often unfair and exhausting. (Try reading the book of Ecclesiastes if you want a picture of someone who had everything, but everything wasn't enough.)

We can never pour enough people, places, or things into our personal cup to keep our lives filled and overflowing with the contentment we want so much. It's no wonder so many people lead lives of emotional desperation, and even consider suicide as a way out.

In fact, by focusing on people, places, and things, we not only miss the positive emotions we want . . . *we end up with the very negative emotions we've been trying all our lives to avoid!* This is true because hurt feelings, worry, anxiety, fear, unrest, uncertainty, and confusion come as a direct result of "expecting" life from a person, place, or thing.

If our ultimate goal in a marriage is saying to our spouse, "I need life from you. Will you cooperate, meet my needs, and fill up my cup?" we're asking for big problems and an empty life.

Many marriages find a husband and wife like two dry sponges, each waiting to soak up life from the other. While we're expecting wisdom, love, peace, and joy from our spouses on a daily basis, they can be sitting across the table expecting us to provide all their needs as well. Then we all come up empty, and major problems can develop.

Why do we get our feelings hurt in the course of an average week? If we're honest and look closely at our circumstances, it's because we've been expecting "life" from someone (or something) who isn't cooperating, and there's one thing more. At the heart of our desperate longing for others to fulfill our deepest needs is a grabbing selfishness that says, "Me first, me first!"

My daughter Kari is a constant source of encouragement to me—and sometimes a loving source of correction as well. I can be frustrated with her over some minor matter and begin to get angry, but she'll always stay incredibly calm. I've often asked her to help me isolate why I'm feeling angry, and she'll say, "Now, Dad, you know that this thing is not really making you angry. It's just revealing your own self-centeredness!"

As much as I hate to admit it, she's generally right! A situation or person doesn't make me angry. I choose to be angry over whatever thing is blocking my goal or frustrating my plan.

We all face the temptation to look to people, places, and things to fill our cup. We're all selfish in wanting others to cooperate in meeting our needs right now. But it's only those who are wise who realize that there is a pathway to freedom from that unfulfilled feeling.

Freedom from Unfulfilled Expectations

Anger, worry, fear, hurt feelings—we wouldn't choose these emotions for anything. Yet we often end up with such feelings starring on our team.

For years, I carried around a great deal of worry and anxiety in my life. At least a part of it came from my background. A few years ago I began to learn what it takes to be completely free from most of the destructive emotions to which I once felt chained. Fear was one of my biggest problems. Here's how it sneaked up on me.

I grew up in a home that was very permissive. Primarily this was because my mother and father lost their first child not long after my mother had given her a spanking. The spanking itself didn't have anything to do with the child's death. A splinter led to an infection and complications that a country doctor and pharmacist in the early forties couldn't heal. Because of the emotional guilt, my mother made my father promise neither one of them would ever discipline us.

This meant that I grew up in a home with no rules. Take dating, for example. Because there were no boundaries in my home, I didn't actually begin my formal dating until the third grade. I did a lot of informal dating before then, but my formal dating started in third grade.

In a climate where "anything goes," my older brothers were left to come up with any "game" they wanted to tease and scare me. One brother loved to wake me up in the middle of the night and stand me up on a chair where he and his friends would laugh at me. He also loved to take his B-B gun and say to me, "I'll give you to *three* to get going." I'd take off as fast as I could because I knew he'd shoot me if I was still in range at the count of three.

He even used to take me out to the middle of a field with his bow and arrow and shoot an arrow up in the air and say, "Scatter!" I never knew where the arrow was coming down, and I was filled with fear and anxiety as I tried to run to safety. Later, every bush became a hiding place to "scare" me. Every time my parents were away was an opportunity to make me jump in some way.

It may seem that all these things were just "childhood games," but they left fearful memories inside my life. While it's hard for me to admit, I was so filled with fear that when I was twenty-four years old I still couldn't take a shower with my eyes closed. I couldn't even stay in a house alone because I'd think I was hearing people breaking in—and I was in graduate school at seminary at the time!

Today, though, it's been almost ten years since I had a fearful thought. Why? Because I've been learning something very specific from God's Word that has taken the fear right out of my life.

Envy, jealousy, comparison. I used to struggle with these emotions constantly, but rarely any more. Why? Because I'm learning how to take these very negative emotions and turn them into a flashing light that illuminates lasting fulfillment. Let me give you an illustration of what I mean.

Using Negative Emotions as Positive Warning Lights in Life

Let's say Dr. Trent and I have just finished our seminar and we've asked Bob, the local chairman, if he'd take us to the airport. As always, we're cutting it close, but if he hurries we'll make the plane just in time.

As we drive to the airport, Bob is having a great time, asking us questions and commenting on how the conference went. He's moving down the highway at a steady clip when suddenly the red light on the dashboard comes on and starts blinking, indicating there's an oil problem with the engine.

I see the light and point it out to Bob right away. After all, this is the last flight out for the day, and we're really anxious to get home to our families.

"Don't worry," Bob assures me. "That thing comes on and off all the time."

Now, though, the light is shining even brighter and is staying on, not flashing. "Bob, are you sure there isn't a problem with your car?" I ask, beginning to wonder if something is actually wrong.

"Naw, nothing to worry about," he says. Just then his engine freezes up, stranding us in the middle of the freeway and causing us to miss our plane.

Actually, Bob had several options when that warning light came on. He could have pulled over and checked the oil, or flagged someone down who could help him fix the problem, or get us to the airport. He could even have done something like this:

When I asked him the second time about the red light on his dash, he could have said, "Gary, do me a favor. Reach into the glove box and hand me that little hammer that's inside there." When I handed him the hammer, he could have taken it and Wham! Wham! Wham!, smashed out the light. "There, now do you feel better? That light won't bother you any more!"

No intelligent person ignores a warning light. It's installed for a purpose. Rather than smash it, you should learn from it. It will alert you to a potential problem. Unfortunately, when it comes to experiencing negative emotions, many people try and "smash them" out of their lives instead of using them as positive warning lights.

Many people feel tremendously guilty when they experience anger, fear, worry, or hurt feelings. I've learned to use them in a positive way. These emotions are actually red lights flashing telling us our focus is in the wrong spot. We're expecting life from the wrong source!

You see, there's a fundamental problem with expecting fulfillment from people, places, and things. These are the *gifts* of life, not the *source* of life. Any time we expect the gifts of life to give us what only God can, we're asking for our cups to be drained of energy and life itself.

Now, when fearful thoughts come into my life, I don't degrade myself for feeling them. I simply say, "Thank You, Lord, for reminding me that you're the only One who can give life." Instead of resenting negative emotions, I can be thankful for their warning-light reminder that I'm looking for something other than the Lord to fill my cup. They can also be the prod that God uses to get us moving in the direction He has chosen for us. How can we learn to harness negative emotions to point us in the right direction?

*P*eople, places and things are the gifts of life, not the Source of life. . . .

Seeking First the Source of Life

When the red lights of negative emotions fill my life, they are all ultimately tied into the same sensor. It's a spiritual sensor that is saying, "Smalley, you're expecting fulfillment from people, places, and things—not from the Lord." I'm focusing on the gifts of life and expecting them to be the Source of life.

Matthew 6:33 gives us a clear direction on what our Source of life should be. "But seek first his kingdom and his righteousness, and all these things will be given you as well." When I give God first place in my life, He promises to meet all my needs.

I try to love God with all my heart. In other words, He's the highest priority in my life. When I focus on Jesus Christ alone as the Source of my life, an amazing thing happens. Because He loves me and actually possesses the wisdom, love, peace, and joy I've always wanted—He alone can fill my cup to overflowing! That's exactly what He promises to do for His children. Ephesians

3:19–20 tells us that " . . . this love . . . surpasses knowledge—that you may be filled to the measure of all the fullness of God." Can you get any more filled than full? Absolutely not.

Do you understand now why very few people can hurt my feelings? Because I'm no longer expecting people to fill my cup, I'm not hurt when they don't respond in a particular way. Even if my wife or a close friend says something to hurt me, it is still a reflection that my focus was on what they could give or take away—not on what God gives.

Whenever those warning lights go off, I thank God for them. Then I pray and ask forgiveness for focusing on something that is less than Himself. Finally, I ask Him alone to fill my life. Psalm 62 says that we are to wait and hope in God alone. He's our rock, our salvation, our rear guard, our hiding place. He's everything we'll ever need!

Think of how many wives are manipulated by husbands from whom they "expect" life and vice-versa. The more we place our expectations on another person, the more control we give them over our emotional and spiritual state. The freer we are of expectations from others—and the more we depend upon God alone—the more pure and honest our love for others will become.

Tapping into a Limitless Source of Power

For twelve chapters we've looked at the various "skills" that can move a marriage from rock bottom right up at the top. We've also been careful to say that communication and intimacy skills alone aren't enough to build the kind of lasting love we all want. Why? Because if we really want a relationship "made in heaven," we must learn to appropriate the power of Heaven—and that power is available through prayer.

The key to powerful prayer is found in Luke 18. When I pray, I become a great deal like the little widow woman pictured in this parable of Jesus. He used her as an example to teach the disciples how to pray. Let me tell her story:

There was once a little old widow lady who went before a wicked judge seeking protection from people who were bothering her. The problem was, this judge had no respect for either God or man, and he repeatedly turned her away. Even with that kind of treatment, she never gave up.

Every day she got in line in front of that wicked judge. Finally, through sheer persistence day after day, she got the protection she was looking for. What was the point of this story? Jesus went on to tell His disciples that we have a God who loves us. "How much more will He hear and answer our prayers" when we line up every day with our requests.

That's how I pray. I line up every day before God and wait expectantly for His answer to my prayers. Of course, even before I pray, I make sure that I'm praying as I should. I always pray keeping 1 Timothy 6:3 in mind, checking to see that my petition is consistent with God's will and that it leads to godliness. If I'm careful that my request meets these standards, then I never get out of line—just like that widow woman. How does this apply to a marriage or having a strong family?

Remember John and Kay Hammer, the couple back in Chapters 1 and 3 who went through such terrible struggles? Kay learned all the "skills" I could teach her about how to have a strong marriage, but that wasn't all. She also learned how to tap into the one power source that could fill her cup to overflowing. That source was separate from anything John could ever do. Once her expectations for wisdom, love, peace, and joy were placed on her God and not her husband, she was finally free to love John. She also had the strength to keep persistently, expectantly praying for positive changes to happen in their relationship.

As she practiced the skills of growing a great relationship, she also prayed continually for a positive result in her home, in her own and her husband's lives. It was her attitude of prayer that gave her the power to keep going when all her feelings said, "Give up!"

Standing in line every day before God reminds me of the story of a man who died and went to heaven. The first place St. Peter took him was to a huge warehouse. It stretched for miles, and it was filled with millions and millions of presents.

"What in the world is this room?" the startled newcomer asked.

"This room is full of presents that were for God's children," Peter answered. "But they got out of line too soon."

I know many, many couples who began the work of forging a loving relationship—but they got out of line too soon. They weren't persistent enough. They ran out of strength to keep their relationship together, forgetting that "those who hope in the Lord will renew their strength" (Isaiah 40:31).

Whenever I wake up in the middle of the night and find my stomach knotted over some problem I'm facing, I've learned to do something that puts me right back to sleep. I've learned to thank God for my knotted stomach, because it's telling me that I'm focusing on one of the gifts of life for love, peace, and joy, rather than the Source of life. The level of my cup doesn't vary now from day to day, phone call to phone call, circumstance to circumstance, because His mercies are new every morning—a fresh full cup of life every day.

It's not Norma who fills my cup. It's not Kari, or Greg, or Michael. It's not my good friends or family members. They're "overflow," not my basic needs. John 17:3 says that to know God is life. Just knowing Christ is life. It's not knowing about Him, it's knowing Him. In 1 John 5:12 the apostle says, "He who has the Son has life; he who does not have the Son of God does not have life." It's as simple as that.

Is your life filled with negative emotions? Or all the fullness of Christ? As we close this chapter, let me share with you one example. I hope it will bring this concept closer to your heart. It did for me the first time I heard Linda's story.

A Single Place to Plug in our Lives

Linda was a young woman who had suffered terribly as a child. Her father adored her, but with his untimely death when she was only five, it seemed she was left without anyone to love her. Her mother resented her, and her brothers and sisters rejected her. All through her childhood, Linda could remember crying herself to sleep at night, wanting so much for things to be different, but they never were.

Linda's desires in life were the same as ours. She longed for others to highly value her. She wanted inner happiness, calm, and contentment. Yet growing up in a negative, non-Christian environment, she experienced only anger, bitterness, and defeat.

Up to this point, I've talked about the Lord filling our cup. Let me change the imagery to give us a different perspective. It was as if Linda's life were a lamp with a single cord.

She wanted desperately to see her life lit up with positive

feelings and a warm, inner calm. She wanted the joy of knowing she was accepted unconditionally by her mother and loved by her brothers and sisters. Yet every time she tried plugging into her family, she received a terrible shock.

Over the years, Linda had been shocked so many times by her family, she sometimes felt like giving up. The very people who should have given her love and acceptance had given her only pain and hurt. Thus she often considered taking her own life.

Linda was so tired of darkness and being shocked, so desirous of light in her life, that she went to another extreme. She spent years plugging into anything and anyone she thought might bring her power and warmth.

She tried lighting her life by plugging into friends, dating, school, jobs, houses, even "recreational" drugs and alcohol. Every time she plugged into one of these things, they, too, left her trapped in darkness and afraid she would never see the light she longed for.

Do you know someone like Linda? Has a difficult background or even some present relationship left you searching for the light of love and peace, and full of darkness and fear? Like Linda, there is only one place where any of us can plug in our lives and find the satisfaction we so desperately need.

Plugging into the Source of Life

When Linda finally discovered that she needed to plug into the Source of Life, Jesus Christ, she saw her life light up for the first time. In His love she found unconditional acceptance (Romans 8:38–39; John 10:1ff; Hebrews 13:5). In His power she found the strength to be joyful in spite of her circumstances (Philippians 4:11–14; 1 Peter 1:6–9). Guided by His hand, she found a spiritual family at a nearby church. They loved her unconditionally. Through His Word and Spirit she received the inner peace that had always eluded her (John 14:6, 1 John 5:1ff).

Perhaps you need to ask yourself what your life is plugged into. Many people try to carry around dozens of "extension" cords and plug them in to the Lord as well as many other people and things, but God has designed us with a single cord and only one place where we can plug it in to find lasting life and power— Himself.

One afternoon after a long conversation with a close friend, Linda made the most significant decision anyone can make. For the first time, she plugged her life into the Source of Life. For the next year and a half, she made a daily decision to look only to the Lord to light up her life.

Whenever she found herself angry with her husband or impatient with her children, she took time to realize that she was really plugging in to them, trying to use them for fulfillment or to meet an unmet need in her own life. Most importantly, whenever she thought about her terrible past and her light began to dim, she would immediately unplug from the hurtful memories and plug back into the positive words of Scripture to discover a special future her Heavenly Father had for her.

What happened when Linda found a single, unbroken source of life to plug into? Her life was never again the same.

Her marriage began to blossom as she finally stopped expecting her husband to make up for years of neglect she had experienced with her family. In her early fifties, she even called her estranged mother and began working to restore that relationship. Her mother was in her eighties!

Linda still met with the same painful, discouraging words, but somehow the shock had been turned off. She was finally free to love her mother because she wasn't expecting anything from her—and it made a major difference in their relationship. She never knew the joy of leading her mother to Christ, but at least Linda was free from the choking feelings of hatred and anger she had carried for years.

Are you expecting life from another person? Someone in the past, like your parents? Someone in the present, like your spouse? Are you struggling with forgiving them because they've "taken" something from you? Something only God could ever have given you in the first place?

For some of us, this single concept of plugging into Christ alone for wisdom, love, peace, and joy can be the most freeing experience in our lives. It certainly was for me.

For me, learning that the ministry, other people, and even my spouse would never fill my cup was the very thing that got me up out of bed when I was so depressed. Believing and practicing the fact that Jesus alone is the Source of life, wisdom, fulfillment, and purpose is what has kept me active and excited about life ever since. I've already accomplished more from a human perspective than I've ever dreamed possible—and in large part it's because I no longer look at life from a human perspective. I'm free to succeed or fail because Jesus Christ is the Source of my life, the fullness of my cup that can never be drained away.

There remains only one final area to discuss before we close this book. In many ways, it could be the most important. In addition to learning that Christ alone could free me from unrealistic expectations, I discovered something else during that difficult time. Even the very trials that led me to depression actually contained valuable gold for developing strong, lasting relationships.

14

The Source of Lasting Love

Some readers may be thinking, *All this talk about having strong relationships and even "plugging" into Christ as my only Source of life is great, it's inspiring. I can even believe it works for other people—but not for me. There's no hope for me.*

I can hear you saying, "You've never met my husband! You've never met my wife! She's been unfaithful! He's left me before! My kids have turned against me! She's turned away from God! I'm a pastor's wife, and I can't tell anyone our problems! I've already been divorced twice! I've had five jobs in the last year and none of them have worked out! . . ."

In almost twenty years of working with individuals, couples, and families, I've heard terrible stories of heartache and tragedy. Many of these certainly sound like "exception" clauses to God's power to turn a terrible situation into something positive. Let me tell you Diane's story:

Diane came to one of our seminars. In her early sixties today, as a young girl she had lived in a very beautiful home in the Northwest. Her father was a well respected attorney in the community, but he was a terror to live with at home. Verbally and sometimes physically abusive, he was always critical and unreachable.

When she was nine years old, her mother caught her father in the midst of an affair. In a fit of anger, she threatened to expose her husband and ruin his reputation in their small town, but like a wounded lion, he turned on her and successfully sued *her* for divorce first—thoroughly slandering her name in the process. Their "soap opera" courtroom theatrics became so bad, other parents forbade their children to play or even talk with Diane or her older brother at school. Then, one day, circumstances turned from bad to far worse than Diane could ever have imagined.

When Diane and her brother came home from school, the movers were in the house packing all their things and getting ready to cart them away. Their father had won the divorce decree and had even gotten a court order evicting his former wife from the house.

As the mother wept, Diane's older brother became furious. He stormed into the house and up to his father's room, grabbing up a gun he knew his father always hid in his bedside drawer.

When he came out of the house, his grandmother was walking up the porch and saw him with the gun. In a burst of anger, he told her he was on his way to kill his father. She grabbed at him, trying to wrestle the gun away. But in the struggle the gun went off. In a terrible accident Diane's brother had killed his own grandmother.

Tragedy would follow tragedy that day. When the police came to the house, they tracked down the boy who was hiding in a neighbor's garage. A gun battle broke out, and an officer was critically wounded. Diane's brother was killed.

Can you imagine her feelings? Only nine years old, she had lived through the trauma of her parents' hostile divorce. She had lost her grandmother and brother in a single day. The community was blaming her because her brother had nearly killed a police officer. And now she was literally put out on the street after having lived in the lap of luxury.

There was nothing good about what happened to this woman or her family. The pain her father and brother caused will always be with her. And yet she told us, "It's taken many years, but I can actually say that God has used my terrible childhood to make me a much better person, especially with my own family. I've had to work through a lot, but I know God has made me a more loving wife and mother because of what I've been through."

Certainly, you say, her story is an exception. Exceptional perhaps, but an exception? Hardly. Here is another story that may be even worse. We share it to underline that whatever we're personally struggling with, if God can turn a situation like this into something worthwhile, He can bring about a similar result in our trials.

Two Roads to the Same Destination

During the Vietnam War, two very different men were part of a Navy SEAL Team, an ultra-elite group sent on dangerous search-and-destroy missions. One was Dave Roever.

Dave would sit on his bunk and strum his guitar, singing religious folk songs and telling his buddies how much God loved them. The other man occupied the bunk above him. His name was Mickey Block, and along with another soldier, he gave Dave a hard time, constantly telling him to shut up and to knock off his preaching. In fact, as in many combat units, they gave Dave a nickname. During his tour in Vietnam, his handle would be the "Preacher Man." Dave came up with his own nickname for them, calling them Pervert Number One and Pervert Number Two!

One night, while on an ambush raid in their heavily armed patrol boat, another American vessel mistook them for the enemy and started firing. Mickey was hit over a dozen times by shrapnel and large caliber machine-gun bullets. His right leg was shot to pieces, and the top of his left hand was torn to the bone by a grenade blast.

The next year and a half, Mickey spent in and out of the hospital in tremendous pain. The doctors tried valiantly to save his leg, but they couldn't. The rest of his body was held together with pins and tubes for months. He found his only relief in getting high, and he stayed that way until he had become addicted to painkillers.

Life moved on at the front, and Mickey heard little about those he had fought with in his SEAL unit, but he did hear about Dave—and he knew he had to be dead.

Not long after Mickey was wounded, Dave was out on a combat mission with a squad of men when they were pinned down by enemy machine-gun fire. Dave pulled a phosphorus grenade from his belt to light up the enemy's position and stood up to throw it, but as he pulled back his arm, a bullet hit the grenade, and it exploded next to his ear.

Lying on his side on the bank of a muddy river in Vietnam, he watched part of his face float by. The rest of his face and his shoulder alternately smoldered and caught fire as the embedded phosphorus came into contact with the night air.

Dave Roever knew that he was going to die, yet miraculously he didn't. He was pulled from the water by his fellow soldiers, flown directly to Saigon, and then taken to a waiting plane bound for Hawaii. But his problems were just beginning.

In the months that followed, he would have dozens of operations—but he almost didn't make it through the first one. The Navy surgical team had a major problem during that operation. As they cut away tissue that had been burned or torn by the grenade, the phosphorus embedded in his body would hit the oxygen in the operating room and begin to ignite again! Several times the doctors and nurses ran out of the room, leaving him alone because they were afraid the flammable oxygen used in surgery would explode! Roever survived that first operation and was taken to a ward that held the most severe burn and injury cases from the war.

The real struggle for both men came after the war. Roever would start each day putting his wig on his bald head, adjusting his false ear, un-taping his eye which has to be taped closed at night since he has no eyelid, and staring at a face that shows the horror of burned flesh. Mickey, at the same time, was surviving skin grafts, amputation, traction, and plastic surgery only to acquire a bone disease and recurring abscesses and infection.

The two had pain and trauma in common after they came home, but beyond that their lives were very different. Mickey would sit in his house at night with a loaded gun in his lap, hoping someone would try to break in so he could shoot the intruder down. His marriage was ruined, and his addictions were getting worse.

Dave, on the other hand, had fallen back on his faith. Soon he was speaking across the country about his experiences. One special night, I heard him speak on national television, and he said: "I am twice the person I was before I went to Vietnam. . . . I wouldn't trade anything I've gone through for the benefits my trials have brought to my life. . . ."

I know what some of you are thinking now. *These people are crazy! How can a trial like this benefit us?* But before you put down the book, read what happened next.

About the same time that Dave Roever was telling how his trials had given him a better spiritual and family life, Mickey Block decided to kill himself. He sat in a chair in his bedroom and stuck his gun in his mouth. Even though he was not a "religious" person to say the least, he recounted that he suddenly felt as if he had seen a vision.

In his mind's eye, he saw the scene a moment after he'd pull the trigger, his brains and blood splattered over the wall behind him. He saw his children come running into his room after school. He tried to get up out of the chair and tell them not to look, but he couldn't! He saw the horror and fear in their eyes as they found his lifeless body slumped in the chair. . . .

As he sat there, a second away from death, he blinked away

the terrible picture of what he had almost done and began crying for the first time since Vietnam. Then, also for the first time, he prayed. He thought back to all the "preaching" he'd heard from Dave Roever and other Christians he had known and finally surrendered what was left of his broken life to Jesus Christ.

What happened next, he would only explain as a peace settling over him. Nothing drastic changed that day. His marriage was still shattered, his leg was still gone. He still battled his addictions, but now there was hope in his life—and a deep inner knowledge that he was forgiven for a life turned against God. He was no longer alone with his problems. His wife viewed his conversion with skepticism but as the months passed, she knew he was a changed man.

Then the day came when a friend called who happened to be listening to a local radio program. "Hey, Mickey," he said. "There's a guy talking about God on the radio who was a member of the SEALs in Vietnam like you were. Do you think you know him?"

The Preacher Man? Mickey thought. It couldn't be. From the account he had heard from the men who put Dave's body on the helicopter in 'Nam, he knew he was dead.

He called the radio station, his hands trembling as he asked to speak to the Vietnam veteran who had just been on the show. After a few moments, a familiar voice came on the line and said, "This is Dave Roever. Can I help you?"

In a few moments of animated conversation, Mickey found out that the "Preacher Man" was in town to speak at a church that night. Dave warmly invited him to attend the meeting, and he agreed. Mickey hadn't been inside a church in years, but that night he went with his wife. By way of introduction he put a .308 caliber machine-gun bullet in the offering plate—the type of bullet they used on their patrol boats and that had torn off his leg.

When the bullet was given to Dave at the front, he stopped speaking and called for his combat buddy to come up with him. Mickey limped the length of the church to Dave's waiting arms, amidst the tears and cheers of the people in the church.

That night, two men stood at the front of that church. They had both lived through the same excruciating, horrible experience. Each had taken a different road to the same destination. One found a deeper faith through having his face nearly blown away. The other lost his leg and nearly his wife and family—but finally he gained everything worth living for. He had new life in Christ and new hope for his family.

Turning Wrong Around

Not one of us would want to experience the kinds of tragedies that Diane, Mickey, and Dave experienced. Yet in each case, these people became stronger in their personal and family lives as a direct result of their trials.

One of the greatest truths I know is that life is difficult and often unfair. What makes the difference between those people who experience difficulties and grow bitter—and those who find a better life produced by a similar or even more difficult trial?

I experience the joy of sharing all across the country that everyone who knows Jesus Christ as Lord and Savior can have the assurance that their trials will produce good in their lives. In fact, for the believer, I often say, every trial comes gift-wrapped with a treasure ready to be found inside.

When Trials Fall from the Sky

I once heard of a man who was walking along the sidewalk outside his high-rise apartment in New York City. It was very early on a bitterly cold winter morning, and he was hurrying to get out of the wind. Suddenly, from out of nowhere, he was hit on the shoulder by a heavy object and knocked to the ground.

For several moments he lay on the sidewalk, dazed, feeling to see if his shoulder was broken. Finally, he sat up and looked around. The street was deserted, so he ruled out a mugging. He looked up at the apartments above him, but he could see no lights on and no open windows. He glanced around the ground where he was lying and saw a shoe box next to him. It was heavily taped from end to end. He reached over to pick it up, but it was so heavy he had to use both hands.

He took the shoe box back to his apartment, got some scissors out, and cut through the tape. Inside were three fairly large cloth sacks. As he lifted out one of the sacks and opened it in the light he gasped. There were several small gold bars and dozens of gold coins! After a few more moments of gasping, he decided he'd better take this shoe box to the police station.

The police told him that more than likely the gold was stolen jewelry that had been melted down. Whether it had fallen from an apartment or from a plane overhead, they couldn't say. If he'd leave it with them for six months, they told him, it could be his if no one lawfully claimed it during that time.

The six months took forever to pass, but finally the day came. He hurried to the police station and there was the shoe box that had given him the sore shoulder. His shoulder didn't hurt anymore, and soon because of this treasure that fell from nowhere, his pocketbook didn't either.

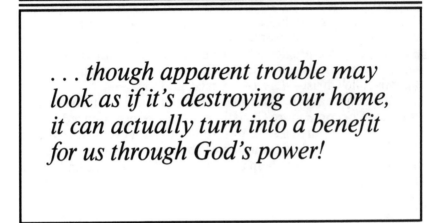

... though apparent trouble may look as if it's destroying our home, it can actually turn into a benefit for us through God's power!

Most of us would gladly suffer through a sore shoulder to end up with a box filled with gold. Yet we may not realize that we have the same chance of benefiting every time we are hit by problems. For every trial is like a box containing valuable treasures. It may knock us to the ground and bruise us, but once we learn how to open the box, we can find a golden opportunity inside.

"Gary, you're either crazy or oversimplifying the problem of pain," some may say. "It's hard to believe that every problem can have a silver lining." After all, what good can come from some serious trial? A trial like having your face nearly blown away? Or from losing your leg and being on drugs? Or from being put out on the street at age nine?

As Diane, Dave, Mickey, Joni Eareckson Tada, Corrie Ten Boom, and many others can testify, trials are often devastating at the time. Yet in spite of the pain, they can produce a gold of sorts in our lives. Like a refining fire, each trial can work to make us more pure and sound. The Bible says God will " . . . bestow . . . a crown of beauty instead of ashes . . ." (Isaiah 61:3).

Don't misunderstand me. I'm not implying that God causes all trials (James 1:13). Neither am I saying that we ought to cause trials for others so that they'll gain from the experience (Romans 6:1–2). But I certainly do believe that in His sovereignty and love, God *can and does* take anything that happens to us and use it for good (Romans 8:28; Isaiah 61:7).

It isn't wrong to avoid painful situations when possible, but it is wrong to deny problems, ignore them, or try to explain them away. As Christians, we are left with a much more positive option than denial or trying to delude ourselves into thinking tragedies didn't happen. Of all people we have a promise that whether we get blasted in the jungles of Vietnam, or in the front yard of our father's home, trials can produce the very things that can make us the most like Christ—His love, peace, and joy.

It's never easy to "welcome" trials as friends, but trials can train us to become more Christlike, if they're experienced in the right light. I've learned to "treasure-hunt" with every difficulty I face. This attitude has been one of the most important tools we can give our children to help prepare them for the large and small trials of life they'll inevitably face.

How God Turns Trials into Triumph

I'm writing this chapter because I know that trials can not only defeat individuals, they can ruin entire families—especially if that family doesn't know how to handle the trials effectively. So here's a summary of this entire book in three sentences.

In Chapters 1 through 12, there's a practical plan we can follow to strengthen our relationships and develop the specific skills necessary to practice that plan. In Chapter 13, we looked at the only consistent power source—the Lord Jesus Himself. Only He can give me the strength to love my spouse as I should over a lifetime. *Now in this final chapter, we have the assurance that although apparent trouble may look as if it's destroying our home, it can actually turn into a benefit for us through God's power!*

That means all trials, over all seasons of the life-cycle. Let me give you a personal example. I'll take you on a treasure-hunting journey through three of my own personal trials and show you the benefits that God ultimately gave me through each one. We'll begin with a trial I faced early in life. It has left a lasting mark upon me.

Being Held Back Moved Me Forward

Until I was in high school, I had moved at least once every year of my life. I'm not proud to admit it, but between bouncing in and out of so many different schools, I flunked the third grade. A number of children are held back before or after kindergarten at an age when it's socially acceptable, but how do you explain to your friends that you're being held back in the third grade because you can't read well enough?

While it may not make anyone's list of all-time trials, I can assure you that at the time, it was one of the greatest traumas I had ever faced. Now, as I look back years later, what did I get from the experience? Humility, to begin with.

Not being promoted with my friends kept me humble for many years. To this day I am self-conscious about my spelling. That's especially true if I have to write a note to one of my children's teachers, because my atrocious spelling was one of the reasons I was held back. Humility may not sound like such a great benefit, but a valuable gift of gold can be added to our character as a result of being humbled. It's found in a verse that says, "God opposes the proud but gives grace to the humble" (James 4:6). While I didn't realize it at the time, God was actually giving megadoses of His grace to me during the third grade!

Flunking third grade also made it difficult for me to read aloud in front of people. One of my most embarrassing moments was the time I was not able to finish reading a section of Scripture at my church. As president of a large college group, I was humbled even more by that experience. It gave me a deep concern for those struggling with dyslexia and other spelling and reading disorders such as mine.

Also, because I was so embarrassed, to this day I am extremely careful to try not to embarrass people who attend my seminars. My experience of embarrassment increased my sensitivity. This is also a fundamental requirement for being a loving person.

At the time I didn't feel there was anything good about flunking a grade, but there was. I received more of God's grace and added sensitivity to hurting people. Two major benefits from one trial, and that's just one trial.

When Our Ship Came In . . . and Ran Aground

During our first few years together, Norma and I lived on the edge of poverty most of the time. My poor accounting skills didn't help.

One year, we had absolutely no money—but we could see our ship coming in any day! Especially since we knew that a tax refund of $2,000 was on its way to us in the mail. When the letter came from the IRS, I hurriedly ripped it open, certain that I'd find a check inside that would be a tremendous help to us financially. Instead, I learned that I had made a major error on our tax form and that we actually *owed* the government $1,700—and they wanted it *now!*

At the time, I couldn't think of a single treasure I was getting out of this particular trial. In fact, I was dying trying to come up with every cent of earthly treasure we had, just to keep the Federal agents away from our door. As Norma and I look back on that experience, however, the real treasure didn't go to the government to play catch-up with the deficit. We learned several lessons more important than money, and they have stayed with us until this day.

The first benefit was the reminder that money is not the source of life. We had focused on our tax refund so much, it had shifted our focus away from Christ. That experience took away everything we had monetarily in life, but God showed us that neither money nor anything money could buy could take away what was more important—our relationship with Him. Because we had to struggle so much to pay the tax bill, the whole family learned the value of trusting God to meet our needs. (Including things like saying "thank you" for care-packages of food that were delivered mysteriously by some close friends.)

Finally, the trial forced me to get professional help with my taxes so that I wouldn't get any "surprises" in the mail again. It also forced me to take a more serious look at the management of our finances. Trial number two, and this time three major positive benefits by nearly going broke! Actually, I could count even more benefits, especially the love we gained through the experience

—remembering that we gain more of God's love in every trial (Hebrews 12:9ff).

A Matter of Life and Death

When it comes to my third example of treasure-hunting trials, to tell you the truth, I'm glad I'm still around to explain it. While it's not easy for me to talk about, for the last two years, my health has not been the best. Basically, at times I've felt I had one foot in heaven and the other on a banana peel here on earth.

You see, my brother died of a heart attack two years ago at the age of 51. My sister had a heart attack last year as well, and another brother had to have triple bypass surgery at age 51. For those who are believers in genetics, it seems that my father's background may have something to do with the hearts in our family giving out when they do. My father died of a heart attack at age 58.

With my family's health history in mind, something happened two years ago—when I was 46—that started me counting my days.

For years, I've jogged a short distance every day and carefully watched my diet, hoping that alone would keep me healthy and fit. Then one morning in Vail, Colorado, during a speaking visit, I walked out of my hotel for a morning jog. Before me were 50 to 60 people, all in running clothes, stretching out and pinning race numbers on their T-shirts.

Recognizing them as people from the convention I was addressing, I said, "Hey, what are you guys doing?"

"This is the annual three-mile race," several people said. "Why don't you come and join us? Everyone at the convention is invited to run."

"You're only going *three miles?*" I asked.

At the time I could do three miles without breaking a sweat in the near sea-level altitude of Phoenix. So I walked over to the sign-up table, got myself a number and joined in. However, I soon discovered that there was a slight problem. This wasn't the friendly three-mile jog I had envisioned. It was a flat-out sprint through two-mile-high Vail. I was a short-distance jogger, not a long-distance sprinter, but the male conqueror mentality inside me kicked in, and I decided I was not going to finish in last place if it killed me.

It almost did.

Before I reached the half-way point, there were small children and senior citizens passing me. It was as if all the breathable air had suddenly been sucked out of Colorado. As I struggled to reach the finish line, I could see that last place was either going to be me or to a woman wheezing alongside me who looked like she'd flunked out of Weight Watchers. So I gave it all I had at the end—and she beat me.

The moment the race was over, I knew something was terribly wrong. I was sick. I spoke that day, then got on the plane with chills and fever. Before I knew it, I was vomiting and bleeding internally. I spent two weeks in bed and even then my blood pressure and cholesterol levels didn't recover. My kidneys were secreting blood, and I was having massive headaches. They were so bad that one doctor wanted to do surgery on my sinuses to drill holes in them so they could drain. Something about the altitude, my health, and my sprint had turned my body inside out.

What good could come out of almost dying? Particularly when John and I had conferences to conduct and books lined up to write? All this required nonstop work.

In the last two years, I have been forced to learn how to balance my life—how to level out the "high-highs" and "low-lows." I have learned even more about healthy food, healthy eating habits, and healthy work habits. I learned what burn-out and stress can do to a body and how damaging out-of-control emotions can be on my system. I also learned how to seek the Lord in a way I'd never done before.

As I learned the concept I described in Chapter 13 (gaining my fulfillment from Christ). I also re-learned the "little widow lady" attitude of prayer. For months, I had to wait daily in that line for my own physical health and strength and to accept that I may not be able to walk through every door of "ministry" that's open to me. The treasure I've gained from that experience is a clearer understanding of how God does give His strength to the weak and of His faithfulness to those who seek Him alone.

These were three trials at different times in my life, some small and some large. Each resulted in similar gains in my store of God's love, peace, and joy. Herein lies the secret to successful treasure-hunting. We can gain a great deal through our trials or nothing at all—depending on our faith. It's not how *much* faith we have, but whether the faith we have takes God at His Word.

Great Faith or "Dinky" Faith

The secret to successful treasure-hunting is understanding two life-changing words: faith and love. The greater our faith in God's Word, the easier it is for us to treasure-hunt trials. The more we treasure-hunt, the more we'll be able to see the ways we're becoming more loving as a result of our circumstances. It all begins with faith, however. We have to take God at His Word. It's not more faith we need, but great faith. Here's what I mean.

Do you remember the story of the centurion who came to Jesus for the sake of his servant? It's one of the clearest descriptions in the Scriptures of exactly what "faith" entails. Read Luke 7 to see if I'm telling the story correctly.

The centurion was a powerful man who commanded an entire garrison of men. Yet one day he faced a problem he couldn't defeat on his own, and he pushed his way through a crowd until he stood in front of Jesus. Coming quickly to the point, he said, "Sir, my servant is lying paralyzed at home, suffering great pain." Even though the man made only a statement, not a request, Jesus answered, "I will come and heal him."

But do you remember the centurion's response?

"Lord," he said, "I am not worthy for You to come under my roof. I am a man used to giving and taking commands. Just say the word, and my servant will be healed." Amazed by the centurion's faith, Christ said to the people around him, "I have not found such *great faith* with anyone in all of Israel!"

Anyone? He was talking about a very religious country. This Roman soldier had greater faith than anyone Jesus knew? Even greater faith than the disciples who would one day die for Him?

"Have you ever wondered what the disciples must have thought about such a statement? Peter was probably saying under his breath, *Sure, Lord, embarrass us in front of our Jewish brethren!* There was no love lost between the Jews and Roman soldiers.

What had impressed Jesus so much about what the soldier had said?

The answer is like a picture-frame around the concept of faith. This soldier believed that Jesus had only to command it and his servant would be healed. "For I, too, am a man under authority," he said to Jesus, "with soldiers under me; and I say to this one, 'Go!' and he goes, and to another, 'Come!' and he comes, and to my slave, 'Do this!' and he does it" (Matthew 8:10). The centurion never doubted for a moment Christ's power and authority to heal his servant. Jesus had said it, and that settled it in his mind.

But why *didn't* he doubt? Problems in life are so quick to produce questions in most of our minds. Perhaps the centurion's faith came from facing the trials of spending many days, on many different battlefields. Perhaps it was a reflection of his own father's faith. We're never told how this man came about his great faith. In contrast, Christ's disciples showed theirs to be of "dinky" proportions almost immediately.

It had been a long day of speaking to the crowds and healing the sick, when Jesus told His disciples to "get into their boat and cross to the other side of the lake." Exhausted from the drain of the crowd, He lay down to take a nap.

When the disciples were halfway across the sea, a storm blew in. Waves crashed over the sides of the boat and the disciples panicked. In desperation, they woke Jesus and cried out, "We're perishing!" Jesus just sighed, stood up, and quieted the waves and the wind with a single command. Then, drawing on the living illustration of the centurion's faith, He said to His disciples: "Why are you so timid, you men of little faith?"

How did the disciples' faith differ from that of the centurion? Why did a Roman soldier have "great" faith and Christ's own disciples "dinky" faith? The difference was that in the midst of the storm, *the disciples forgot what Jesus had said to them.* They quit counting on His Word, and as a result they panicked and counted themselves in the "lost at sea" category.

Jesus specifically said to them before He went to sleep, "We're going to the other side," not, "You guys better hug everybody, because we're fish-food halfway across this lake." He had given them His word they would *all* cross to the other side. Yet they forgot His words when the water got choppy.

I'm not blaming the disciples—I'm too much like them. Many of us make the same mistake in our marriages and families, don't we? During difficult times. we forget that God promises we'll make it to the other side—He just never promises a smooth ride on the way there. *But as the waves crash around us, God promises He will produce maturity, righteousness, patience, endurance, and love in our lives.*

In James 1:2, the writer told us to "consider it pure joy . . . whenever you face trials" and in 2 Corinthians 5:7, Paul told us to "live by faith, not by sight." So questioning the waves and their effect on our trip through life is like saying, "God's promises don't apply to me. God doesn't understand my situation, so how can any good come out of all this suffering?" (Isaiah 40:27ff.).

We're Not the First to Be "Treasure-Hunters"

One look in the Bible shows story after story of gaining treasure from trials. How would you feel if you were hated by your brothers, sold for pennies into a foreign slave market, framed for adultery, thrown into jail without a trial, and then forgotten by the one person who could have saved you?

Joseph, in the Old Testament, knew what that felt like. Yet what did he say years later, when he, the Pharaoh's right hand man, brought his brothers to Egypt? Even as he forgave them he said, "You intended to harm me, but God intended it for good" (Genesis 50:20).

Adam, Noah, Abraham, Isaac, Jacob, Joseph, Moses, Elisha, Elijah, Jeremiah, David, Solomon, Esther, Ruth, Isaiah, John the Baptist, Peter, Paul, Mary Magdalene, James. . . . on and on the list goes. All these are people with whom we can identify. They all faced trials like we have. Even in cases of "failure" (remember, Elisha and Jonah ran away, Peter denied Christ, Paul persecuted Christ's followers, James deserted Him, etc.), God took tragedy and even "dinky" faith and turned it into eternal treasure.

Blocking Trials from Producing Love

I'll be the first to admit that there is a problem with experiencing trials. Namely, their worth to us often comes on a delayed basis. As the waves are bouncing us around, we are just like the disciples. All we can picture is surviving the immediate, not thanking God for how He's shaping us for eternity.

Remember how long it took the average family to turn disasters into "family glue" in Chapter 12? It often takes several weeks for the family to see those disasters in their true light and begin bonding as a result. The same is true with trials. It took time for Dave Roever to say he was a better man for having a hand grenade blow up in his face. Diane didn't stop crying herself to sleep for months after the tragedy she faced at nine years of age—but healing did come one fateful morning.

Experts say that it takes at least thirty days of consistent repetition before a habit becomes ingrained. In other words, don't give up on treasure-hunting when you're only a few feet from shore. When someone's experiencing a trial, it's natural to go through a stage in which anger or doubt takes over, but making a decision to remain angry or even to dwell on being a "victim" can block you from any positive effects the trial could have on your character.

If I wanted to, I could still be angry at my third grade teacher or my parents for not getting me the help I needed to pass the third grade the first time, but hanging on to resentment would simply act as a roadblock to any benefits God could bring me. I could blame Norma or the "Infernal" Revenue Service for a complicated tax system that nearly bankrupted our family—or I could admit my own mistake and look in faith to what God could teach me in what happened.

I could even hate my father's memory—and question God's wisdom—in giving me his genes that may put an early time limit on the years I have to serve Him. To do so, however, would be to kick and scream at a loving and sovereign—and—unfathomable God. (Remember from Chapter 5: Anger blocks God's working in our lives, so we're only cheating ourselves to hold on to feelings of being a victim.)

There's no earthly reason why Dave, Mickey, and Diane should be happy and fulfilled after what's happened to them—but there is a heavenly one. Solomon once said if we live long enough, we'll all see enough sorrow to knock the joy out of life if we let it (Ecclesiastes 12:1). Embracing the value of our trials and mining the constructive good God can bring from them is the only way I know to keep rejoicing for a lifetime.

Passing down the Faith to "Treasure-Hunt"

As I mentioned earlier in the chapter, there are important personal reasons for learning to treasure-hunt trials, but it doesn't stop there. For those of us who have children, it's vital that we begin teaching them lessons in centurionlike faith at an early age—especially if they seem destined to increase their sensitivity level by being slightly (or decidedly) accident-prone.

For whatever reason, my son Michael wins the "I've-experienced-the-most-natural-and man-made-accidents" award in our family. When he was two weeks old, he almost died from severe stomach problems that required major surgery. For the next several years, he suffered through a series of childhood illnesses and came close to death again.

Once when he was three, I was digging in the back yard and unearthed a yellow-jacket nest. Where was my "award-winning" son standing? Right where the nest fell. He was stung repeatedly before I could get to him. Then in the same year, Mike nearly drowned in a motel swimming pool.

He's suffered through a retainer to enlarge his mouth and then braces to pull his teeth in tighter. At age thirteen, he was in a major car accident. He broke an arm and was showered with so much broken glass, it took the doctors two hours to take out all the glass slivers from the side of his face and from his eyelid. Soon he'll undergo an operation in which he will have to get his jaw broken and reset.

What do you say to a child who has gone through so many trials? Why not let him do the talking? When the doctor told Michael that there would probably be some pain involved in his upcoming operation, Mike said, "Oh, don't worry about it. I've had so much pain in my life that this isn't going to faze me."

When people go through painful experiences, it often seems to enable them to go through future experiences with less trauma, as if they understand the process and the refining fire. Michael had already been through so many things that the automobile accident wasn't that traumatic for him. Even during the two hours they worked to take all the glass from his face, he was calm and joking. A week after the accident, Mike's attitude was still positive when he learned that he'd have to go through the entire summer in Phoenix with a cast on his arm and unable to swim. The same will be true when he has his jaw operation. At age sixteen, he's already an avid, well-seasoned treasure-hunter—and he's needed to be!

Teaching Them to Look for Love in an Unusual Place

When you teach your children what God's Word has to say about troubled times, you're providing a true "lamp unto their feet" for the rest of their trial-ridden life. As John and I explain in detail in our book, *The Gift of Honor,* it all begins with your first reaction during a trial. Calmly comforting them at the beginning of a trial lays the foundation for them to find value in their difficult experiences. It teaches them they can be calm, too.

And how do we remain calm at such a chaotic moment? Calmness comes from our own deep inner confidence in God's abiding care. As we discussed in Chapter 13, it's a deep conviction that will work for good in God's time (Romans 8:28).

Watching Mike's positive attitude through his pain gave us an opportunity to praise him for the way he was handling the situation. Yet we made a mental note to keep tabs, as the months went by, on how he was responding (a bit like watching for aftershocks of an earthquake). By doing so, we'd be able to spot early warning signs like depression or anxiety that could grow into major problems later on. That is a good idea for all parents as they smooth the path toward finding the treasure of their children's trials.

Biblical principles are like powerful beacons that can light up even the darkest trial your children may experience. Teaching your children that Romans 8:28 and Philippians 4:1ff speak of spiritual benefits they can claim in faith is a precious legacy you can leave your loved ones. If you take God at His Word yourself, you'll verbally and nonverbally convey this message to your children as they watch your responses to your own troubles.

Great faith is confidently knowing that what God promises will come true. Great faith is the confidence even during a trial that it will one day turn out to our benefit. "Dinky" faith is complaining or "murmuring" during a trial that there is no benefit on the other side, we're doomed. . . . finished . . . beyond help . . . unrepairable. . . .

I firmly believe that the mark of a person who grows through trials is the degree to which he or she is willing to take God at His Word. That is called great faith in the love of God, and only possible for those who . . .

Don't Bail out of the "Love Boat" When Trials Hit

As we've mentioned, the most precious treasure we discover as we unwrap any trial is gaining more of Christ's love. Troubled times have a way of funneling the love and care of God to us, and the love of God *through* us, to others. Only those who desire God's best, His love, truly benefit from trials. Trials are coming to all of us, and it's crucial that we learn to use them for good, rather than let them get us down.

In the weeks after Mike's accident, I sat down with him several times and discussed some of the benefits that were a part of his trial. Because we've done this with so many of his trials, he jumped in quickly, telling me he could see the ways in which he had already become more sensitive. No longer could he pass an accident site and not begin praying for the people instead of just "looking" at what happened.

There's no question in our home about who is the most sensitive family member. No one feels the hurt of people or even animals as deeply as Mike does, and I believe it has everything to do with how much he has suffered.

Recently, on the way to a doctor's appointment, I asked Mike what he wants to do in life. Do you know what he said? "I think I want to try to help protect people somehow. Maybe I'll be a policeman or in some kind of service organization. Maybe I can be a secret service agent or something. I want to do something to help protect people somehow."

How often in our own lives has someone ministered to us during a difficult time with caring eyes and loving ways—and later we learned that person had been through the same kind of problem? One of the clearest treasures a trial offers us is to make us loving and sensitive in its wake. That wonderful sensitivity is, I believe, a major factor in genuinely loving others. We develop more patience, tolerance, sensitivity and over all we become better lovers of people (Romans 5:3–5).

The apostle Paul understood this mystery when he wrote his famous explanation of love: "Love is patient, love is kind. It does not envy, it does not boast, it is not proud. It is not rude, it is not self-seeking, it is not easily angered, it keeps no record of wrongs. Love does not delight in evil but rejoices with the truth. It always protects, always trusts, always hopes, always perseveres" (1 Corinthians 13:4–7).

These qualities of mature love are given to us through trials better and faster than any other way I know. Trials put us in a "love boat" with Jesus. As the disciples we're able to ride out the storm. Just as with them, it's our choice whether we're going to take Jesus at His Word and believe He'll take us to the "other side" of the trial—and gain more love for Him and others in the process. Or whether we'll wake Him up continually with our cries of mistrust and "dinky" faith—and hear His gentle reproof, "Oh, ye of little faith . . . "

I know I can't keep trials from coming. The Bible promises me that trials will show up on my doorstep (James 1:2ff.). Over the years, though, I'm finally coming to the place where I've quit fighting something the Bible says can "Purify you and make you lacking in nothing" (James 1:4).

*T*he qualities of mature love are given to us through trials better and faster than any other way I know . . .

Another way to look at trials is to treat them like long-term "interest-bearing" CDs. It may take time for them to mature and for God to produce a greater capacity to love through our trial, but there's a promise we can count on. We can take Him at His Word that we can cash in on that love one day. As the writer to the Hebrews says, no one enjoys trials, "No discipline seems pleasant at the time, but painful. Later on, however, it produces a harvest of righteousness and peace for those who have been trained by it" (Hebrews 11:11).

A Promise by Day and by Night

Faith is trusting that God's Word is reliable. If He promises, "We are going to the other side," then we are going to the other side. There are a number of promises in the Scripture that can keep us going, keep us searching for that buried treasure of love with a full and open heart. In fact, here's a quick list I offered in the book, *Joy That Lasts* [1] that contains just a few of the promises to remember as trials come to us day by day. I strongly urge you to memorize a list of scriptural promises like these, so that when the next trial hits—you'll stay in His "love boat" and be able to treasure-hunt more quickly when you reach the other side.

1. "And we know that in all things God works for the good of those who love him, who have been called according to his purpose" (Romans 8:28).

2. "Give thanks in all circumstances, for this is God's will for you in Christ Jesus" (1 Thessalonians 5:18).

3. "Consider it pure joy, my brothers, whenever you face trials of many kinds, because you know that the testing of your faith develops perseverance" (James 1:2–3).

4. "Our fathers disciplined us for a little while as they thought best; but God disciplines us for our good, that we may share in his holiness. No discipline seems pleasant at the time, but painful. Later on, however, it produces a harvest of righteousness and peace for those who have been trained by it" (Hebrews 12:10–11).

5. "Jesus replied: 'Love the Lord your God with all your heart and with all your soul and with all your mind.' This is the first and greatest commandment. And the second is like it: 'Love your neighbor as yourself.' All the Law and the Prophets hang on these two commandments" (Matthew 22:37–40).

6. "The goal of this command is love, which comes from a pure heart and a good conscience and a sincere faith" (1 Timothy 1:5).

7. "Dear friends, since God so loved us, we also ought to love one another. No one has ever seen God; but if we love each other, God lives in us and his love is made complete in us" (1 John 4:11–12).

8. Last, but certainly not least, is my favorite chapter in Scripture as I've gone through physical trials this year (Romans 5). To offer a paraphrase of these verses: "Therefore we have been made right with God through faith, peace with God through Christ, and enjoy the power of God in us through Christ. Not only do we have all we need in Him, but we can also be excited about our sufferings. Because trouble brings us endurance—the power to keep going—and endurance produces character (love), character brings hope, and we won't be disappointed (great faith)

because God will pour out His love in our hearts through His Spirit!"

So the truth remains: No one likes trials, yet no one can escape them. We can let them ruin our lives, allowing ourselves to become bitter, angry, resentful. Or we can look for the treasure that will let us love and serve our family and others better. Again, the choice is ours. *For loving God—like loving one's spouse and children—is first, last, and always a decision.*

Notes

Chapter 1

1. In the years ahead, our goal as a ministry is to produce small group follow-up materials that will provide families everywhere with biblically based resources to strengthen their most important relationships.
2. "Even youths grow tired and weary, and young men stumble and fall; but those who hope in the Lord will renew their strength . . ." Isaiah 40:30–31.

Chapter 2

1. Gary Smalley and John Trent, Ph.D., *Hardside/Softside* (Pomona, CA: Focus on the Family Publishers, to be released Spring, 1990).
2. From a training booklet by Jack Hilger, *Training Married Couples to Work with Premarital Couples,* Prepare/Enrich, Inc., 1987.
3. Joan Druckman, David Fournier, Beatrice Robinson, and David H. Olson, "Effectiveness of Five Types of Pre-marital Programs," *Education for Marriage* (Grand Rapids, MI, 1979). Gerald Cossitt, *Effects of Feedback on Idealism in Premarital Couples,* Doctoral dissertation, University of Alberta, Edmonton, Canada.
4. The biblical concept of "honoring" God and others is so important, Dr. John Trent and I wrote an entire book on the subject called *The Gift of Honor* (Nashville, TN: Thomas Nelson Publishers, 1987).
5. Reading books like Frank Peritti's *This Present Darkness* (Westchester, IL: Good News Books/Crossway Publishers, 1988) can help you believe that there may be a satanic cover-up of honor!
6. William F. Arndt and R. Wilbur Gingrich, eds., *A Greek-English Lexicon of the New Testament and Other Early Christian Literature* (Chicago: University of Chicago Press, 1957), 119.
7. Ibid., 120.
8. Men are motivated by the "awe" principle both negatively and positively. One major reason for the creation of affairs is that a woman outside the marriage will show a man "ah-h-h-h-h," and it draws him after her. See Proverbs 5, 6:20–35, and Chapter 7 for a picture of the adulteress who "flatters with her words" in working her destruction.

9. *The Gift of Honor,* Chapter 3.
10. For more on the tremendously damaging effects of negative word pictures, see Gary Smalley and John Trent, Ph.D., *The Language of Love* (Pomona, CA: Focus on the Family Publishing, 1988), Chapter 15, "The Dark Side of Emotional Word Pictures."

Chapter 3

1. For a long overdue look at the long-term negative effects of divorce on children, see the chilling book, Judith Wallenstein, *Second Chances* (New York: Ticknor and Fields Publishers, 1989); Diana Medved, *The Case Against Divorce* (New York: Donald I. Fine, Inc., 1989), and especially, Gary Richmond, *The Divorce Decision* (Waco, TX: Word Books, 1988).

Chapter 4

1. Allen P. Ross, *Creation and Blessing* (Grand Rapids, MI: Baker Book House, 1988), 126.
2. Robert Kohn, "Patterns of Hemispheric Specialization in Pre-Schoolers," *Neuropsychologia,* 12:505–12.
3. James J. Lynch, *The Language of the Heart* (New York: Basic Books, Inc., 1985).
4. For a definition of "word picture," see *The Language of Love,* 17.
5. Arthur Bragg, "What's Holding Them Back?" *Business Insurance* (March 1989).

Chapter 5

1. Leprosy was such a dreaded disease that one rabbi taught it was all right to throw stones at lepers to keep them "a safe distance away," cf. Alfred Edershiem, *The Life and Times of Jesus the Messiah* (Grand Rapids, MI: William B. Eerdmans Publishing, 1971), 1:495.
2. See *aphieimi,* which has the basic meaning of "let go, send away, cancel, remit, pardon, leave, let go, tolerate," Ardnt and Gingrich, *Lexicon,* 125–26.
3. In *The Blessing,* we discuss the physiological benefit of elevated hemoglobin levels in both people involved in the meaningful touch. When elevated, the hemoglobin levels serve to carry more oxygen to our bodies and actually energize us. For more information, see

Gary Smalley and John Trent, *The Blessing*, p. 40, and "Therapeutic Touch: The Imprimatur of Nursing," *American Journal of Nursing* (May 1975): 784.

Chapter 6

1. For a detailed description of the concept of "closing" or "reopening" a person's spirit, see Gary Smalley, *The Key to Your Child's Heart* (Waco, TX: Word Publishing, 1984).
2. For a detailed look at the negative physiology of anger, see Paul Meier and Frank Minirth, *Happiness Is a Choice* (Grand Rapids, MI: Baker Book House, 1978).
3. Ibid., 23–29.
4. Albert A. Kurtland, "Biochemical and Emotional Interaction in the Etiology of Cancer," *Psychiatric Research Review* 35 (1978): 25.
5. "They can sit through sermon after sermon about forgiveness in church, never once misunderstanding what the pastor says, but still refuse to put their son's or daughter's picture back on the mantle." From Gary Smalley and John Trent, Ph.D., *The Blessing* (Nashville, TN: Thomas Nelson Publishers, 1986), 137.
6. We're using "soul" here in a nontheological way and especially not in the way some new-age people would call a "floating soul" touching another.
7. For a more complete list, see Gary Smalley, *If Only He Knew* (Grand Rapids, MI: Zondervan Publishing House, 1979), Chapter 5, "Climbing Out of Marriage's Deepest Pit," 82–86.
8. For an excellent resource on dealing with strong-willed children, see James Dobson, Ph.D., *The Strong-Willed Child* (Wheaton, IL: Tyndale House, 1979).

Chapter 7

1. There are, unfortunately, exceptions. See Gary Smalley and John Trent, Ph.D., *The Language of Love*, "The Dark Side of Emotional Word Pictures" (Pomona, CA: Focus on the Family Publishing, 1988), 150–62; and M. Scott Peck, M.D., *People of the Lie* (New York: Simon and Schuster, 1983).
2. We'll talk about this more later, but physically, emotionally and spiritually a man benefits by developing relationship skills.
3. From the Greek verb, *epitrepho*. Ardnt and Gingrich, *Lexicon,* 343.

Chapter 8

1. For a very helpful resource on leaving your children a legacy of love, see Tim Kimmel, *Legacy of Love: A Plan for Parenting on Purpose* (Portland, OR: Multnomah Press, 1989).
2. For more information on this outstanding conference, contact the Campus Crusade Family Ministry in Little Rock, AR (501) 223–8663.
3. For an insightful, biblically based book dealing with sexual temptation, see Charles Mylander, *Running the Red Lights* (Ventura, CA: Regal Books, 1986).
4. Ibid.
5. For more information about our #1 favorite Christian sports camp for any youngster aged eight to eighteen, please contact Kamp Kanakuk, Route 4, Box 2124, Branson, MO 65616, (417) 334–2432 or 334–6427.

Chapter 9

1. In fact, one of our favorite marriage books is by our good friends, Chuck and Barb Snyder. It's called *Incompatibility: Grounds for a Great Marriage* (Sisters, OR: Questar Publishers, 1988).
2. This is such an important concept, Dr. Trent and I have written an entire book about it called *The Language of Love* (Pomona, CA: Focus on the Family Publishers, 1988).
3. James Ford Rhodes, *History of the United States*. Vol. 1: *Lectures on the American Civil War* (1913). On meeting her, Lincoln reportedly said, "So this is the little lady who wrote the book that made this big war!"
4. Even though you may not realize it, you probably have been using them all your life. Expressions like "I'm toasty warm," "His elevator doesn't go all the way to the top floor!" or "That went over like a lead balloon" are just three of the hundreds of word pictures that are a part of our everyday speech.

Chapter 10

1. H. Norman Wright, *Romancing Your Marriage* (Ventura, CA: Regal Books, 1987), 41.
2. Alice Chapin, *Four Hundred Ways to Say I Love You* (Wheaton, IL: Living Books, Tyndale House Publishers, Inc., 1981).
3. *Romancing Your Marriage.*

4. Dan Carlinsky, *Do You Know Your Wife?* (Los Angeles, CA: Price, Stern, and Sloan, 1984).

Chapter 11

1. Marc H. Hollender, "The Wish to Be Held," *Archives of General Psychiatry* 22 (1970):445.
2. This survey of several thousand women was conducted by Ann Landers and its findings are recorded in "Is Affection More Important Than Sex?" *Reader's Digest* (August 1985).

Chapter 12

1. See chapter 6 for more on "closing" a person's spirit.
2. If you're interested in contacting Bill to do a family enrichment event at your church or business, you can contact him at P.O. Box 2929, Grass Valley, CA 95945, (916) 447-7738.
3. John Piper, *Desiring God* (Portland, OR: Multnomah Press, 1986).

Chapter 13

1. See Proverbs 7:1ff for a chilling description of the high cost of immoral relationships.

Chapter 14

1. Gary Smalley, *Joy That Lasts* (Grand Rapids, MI: Zondervan Publishing House, 1987).